Your Towns and Cities in the (

Ironbridge
in the Great War

This book is respectfully dedicated to all the Ironbridge-area service personnel who were sacrificed to a futile war.

Your Towns and Cities in the Great War

Ironbridge
in the Great War

Christopher W A Owen

Pen & Sword
MILITARY

AN IMPRINT OF PEN & SWORD BOOKS LTD.
YORKSHIRE - PHILADELPHIA

First published in Great Britain in 2018 by
Pen & Sword Military
An imprint of
Pen & Sword Books Ltd
Yorkshire – Philadelphia

ISBN 978 1 78346 400 5

A CIP record for this book is available from the British Library

Printed and bound in England
by CPI Group (UK) Ltd, Croydon, CR0 4YY
Typeset in Times New Roman
by Aura Technology and Software Services, India

Pen & Sword Books Ltd incorporates the imprints of
Pen & Sword Archaeology, Atlas, Aviation, Battleground, Discovery,
Family History, History, Maritime, Military, Naval, Politics, Railways,
Select, Social History, Transport, True Crime, Claymore Press,
Frontline Books, Leo Cooper, Praetorian Press, Remember When,
Seaforth Publishing and Wharncliffe.

For a complete list of Pen & Sword titles please contact

PEN & SWORD BOOKS LIMITED
47 Church Street, Barnsley, South Yorkshire, S70 2AS, England
E-mail: enquiries@pen-and-sword.co.uk
Website: www.pen-and-sword.co.uk

Or
PEN AND SWORD BOOKS
1950 Lawrence Rd, Havertown, PA 19083, USA
E-mail: Uspen-and-sword@casematepublishers.com
Website: www.penandswordbooks.com

Contents

Acknowledgements

To those parties and organisations listed below who made this book possible, with special thanks to the following for their help:

Ironbridge Gorge Museum Trust Library staff, and registrar Joanne Smith, for local industrial history and the use of copyrighted period photographs

Janet Doody, local historian, for local history contributions

Martin Scholes, journalist, ex-*Wrekin News Magazine* – for factual material

Mr Ronald Miles, historian, for his contribution of family documents and stories

Rev Ian Naylor, priest in charge, Holy Trinity Church, Coalbrookdale, for historical material about the church and associated local serving men

Mrs Diane Browne, headmistress of Adcote School, for all her help with the background to the Darby/Arthur family plus use of photo material supplied

Mr David Mumford, warden of St Martin's Church, Little Ness, for his cooperation and help with the contribution to the history of the Darby family in the First World War

Lieutenant Colonel T.J. Boxall and R.M. Millward, Wrekin District Roll of Honour (biographies)

(All permissions and copyrights sought and agreed for materials reproduced here)

List of Abbreviations

AEF	**American Expeditionary Force**
ANZAC	**Australian & New Zealand Army Corps**
BEF	**British Expeditionary Force**
DORA	**Defence of the Realm Act (1914 amended 1915)**
KSLI	**King's Shropshire Light Infantry (regiment)**
The *Journal*	***The Wellington Journal & Shrewsbury News***
VAD	**Volunteer Aid Detachment (Nursing auxiliary)**

Introduction

It is now more than a century since the outbreak of the 'war to end all wars'. It was contested over four and a half bitter and bloody years commencing, for the UK, at 11pm on 4 August 1914 and officially ending at 11am on 11 November 1918.

Such was the carnage resulting from this – the first mechanised global war – that this legendary date is still commemorated every year in London and in little towns like Ironbridge all over the UK. It is known as Armistice Day along with its companion Remembrance Sunday, held on the nearest Sunday to that date.

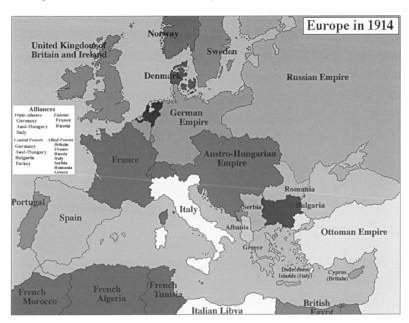

Scale map of European military alliances, circa 1914

Ironbridge area was to suffer some 107 recorded fatalities, thus paying a terrible price for its patriotism. In this book we will discover what this entailed for some of those locally enlisted combatants and their families. We shall include their material sacrifices suffered at home and in the aftermath, the memorials raised in tribute to the fallen in Ironbridge and the four surrounding villages.

The 'Great War' was also called the 'People's War' because it was fought and won mainly by the UK's ordinary working classes. They joined as voluntary or conscripted enlistees, as did the majority of those from the Ironbridge area, who then might find themselves fighting alongside peers of the realm.

Most major world nations were soon drawn into what was to eventually cost an estimated 31 million casualties, civilian and military. Britain was to suffer 870,000 dead, 3 million wounded, and the rest captured or listed as missing in action bringing the total to some 4.7 million. These statistics do not include subsequent deaths from war-related injuries possibly occurring many years after the cessation of hostilities. Over 44 per cent of those enlisted in UK forces were either killed, injured, captured or missing with no known grave.

The total recorded British fatality figures rises to 1.3 million when we include Commonwealth service personnel fighting under the British Empire's flag.

The 108 listed fatalities for Ironbridge excludes the number of captured servicemen. We will include local soldiers whose stories of captivity are recounted in this book for the first time, as well as the winner of a Victoria Cross.

Details of all war-related fatalities are shown in the A-Z listings of local service personnel casualties shown in the back of this book. For anyone researching their family history this would be a useful first resource tool.

Britain, France and Russia were matched against the main antagonists of Germany, Austria-Hungary, Italy, Bulgaria and Turkey. The war did not suddenly erupt spontaneously from nowhere. It had been brewing for many years across a Europe which had become a seething cauldron of fermenting skirmishes and localised wars, particularly in the Balkans.

Using the pretext of the assassination in Sarajevo of Archduke Franz Ferdinand, heir to the Austro-Hungarian Empire and Germany's main ally, Kaiser Wilhelm II invaded Belgium. Britain's response took the form of a declaration of intent which was delivered by the UK's ambassador, Sir Edward Goschen, as a final note to the German Government in Berlin at 10pm on 4 August specifying a two-hour response deadline. The note bluntly demanded that unless Germany unconditionally removed its troops from Belgium a state of war would exist. Receiving no such undertaking, Britain found itself at war with Germany at 11pm on 4 August – midnight in Berlin. The Liberal coalition government under Prime Minister Herbert Asquith believed that this would force Germany to retreat and rethink its actions now the British Empire had thrown its weight behind the Triple Entente agreement in support of an invaded treaty nation. Having already begun their Schlieffen war plan (devised circa 1908) to invade and rapidly conquer French forces via Belgium, the German High Command were faced with the prospect of fighting a war on two fronts. To offset this they engaged their allies Albania and Ottoman Turkey to help keep Russia and its forces pinned down in the east.

Surprisingly most European nations including the UK were unprepared for any coordinated response to the anticipated actions of their German aggressors, which would have possibly prevented warfare altogether. This omission was to prove costly for Britain whose forces found themselves in action on most of the various war fronts worldwide. The strength of what was to become known as the Western Front was well-matched with the German/Austro-Hungarian Axis and their allies, being approximately 150 divisions each.

The land armies soon suffered heavy losses and by the end of 1914 were forced into a stalemate. A war of attrition resulted in a line of defensive trenches stretching across Europe from the Belgian seaboard to the Swiss Alps covering some 600 kilometres. Much of the war in Europe was to remain static and trench-bound for the next four years with small gains contested by both sides only to be later lost in counter-attacks.

In this book we will describe the changes the war brought to Britain and the Ironbridge-area civilians who were to make great sacrifices to help support the fighting men at the front and 'make do' in the face of increasing domestic shortages which led to officially-imposed rationing. The country at this time imported two-thirds of its domestic requirements and the German U-boat blockade of the Atlantic directed against UK shipping caused losses in excess of 5,000 tonnes per month from 1916 onwards.

Industries in the Ironbridge area were among the first to recruit women workers. The war was to fundamentally affect female employment in the British economy. Due to male conscription in 1916, the heavier industries, particularly those war-related, rapidly reached critical levels of manpower. We will detail this first use of female labour in Coalbrookdale to help the war initiative.

In 1917 Russia was eliminated from the war by violent internal revolution, and the tide of the war now turned in Germany's favour as she concentrated the bulk of her troops onto the Western Front. Over-confidence was to dominate the strategy of the German High Command from March 1918 onwards, leading to a series of catastrophic mistakes which lost them the war.

All of this was to come for the denizens of Ironbridge (and its satellite villages) in 1914, a sleepy little town located in rural Shropshire. They basked in the early-August bank holiday sunshine of another world, a peaceful time, that was to end forever in the fires of warfare. Their tranquil thoughts were a million miles away from considering the consequences of being engulfed in the global cataclysm that was shortly to befall them.

CHAPTER 1

1914: Men of Iron

'In the beginning God created Iron ore, and Bedlam men smelted it.'
(Local saying)

Introduction to Ironbridge

Ironbridge is some forty miles north-west of Birmingham, three miles from junction 7 which is the western terminus of the M54 motorway.

View of Ironbridge town – present day

This historical town is located in a semi-rural part of Shropshire, one of the largest farming counties in the West Midlands. It nestles in the basin of the great gorge of the Severn river which snakes lazily eastwards across the south edge of the great Shropshire plain. It then carves its way through dense limestone hills at Buildwas to form the natural gorge leading up to the town itself.

The Severn was once the lifeblood of the community being first and foremost a major transport artery serving all the local industrial village communities along its banks. Up to the late nineteenth century shallow draft sail barges called 'Trows' carried Ironbridge's iron products, pottery and ceramic tiles along the Severn to an eagerly waiting world market. Ironbridge became an industrial heartland containing famous factories producing cast-metal products, fine ceramics of bone china, and decorative tiles, all of them world-famous names.

At the time of the Great War, the town was still referred to in written accounts by the old name of Iron-Bridge, not spelled as one word, possibly in deference to its industrial heritage.

The town itself should not be considered as just the core urban layout clustered around the famous bridge that we see today, but as a conglomeration of smaller villages and hamlets contained within a three-mile radius. They all shared both in the industrial prosperity of the area, and the tragedy of the Great War.

Ironbridge became the focus of huge industrial advancement in the eighteenth and nineteenth centuries. It commenced with the construction of the world's first cast-iron bridge from which the town derives its name.

It was built by the famous ironmasters Abraham Darby III and John Wilkinson (described as 'iron mad') in partnership with several Broseley businessmen.

Construction began in 1779 and it was opened to the public in 1781 as a toll road bridge. Tolls for crossing the Iron Bridge were collected up to 1950 since when it has been closed to vehicular traffic. It was scheduled as an Ancient Monument by act of Parliament in 1934. It is now designated a world heritage site currently under the stewardship of English Heritage (conservators

The Iron Bridge, opened in 1781

charitable trust) in partnership with the local authority, Telford &
Wrekin Council. At the time of going to press it is undergoing a two
million pound renovation (partly crowd-funded) in order to protect
and preserve it for posterity. The town's glory days are now long
gone; Ironbridge town is reduced to the status of a village suburb in
the massive urban sprawl designated as Telford New Town.

The Ironbridge demographic in the Great War
The satellite villages of Ironbridge were still attached for socio-
economic and historical reasons at the turn of the twentieth-
century. For the purposes of consideration regarding the Great War,
these comprise Coalbrookdale, Coalport, Jackfield, Madeley and of
course the main town itself.

Coalbrookdale village

Still busy with industry, Coalbrookdale is located on the same bank of the Severn to Ironbridge in an accompanying gorge running at ninety degrees to the river at the junction of Dale End and the Wharfage near the old Merrythought factory. Its long slow winding road leads us steadily uphill through the village itself past the Ironbridge Iron & Steel Museum Trust complex (originally the Dale Company site) and via Jiggers Bank up to the island on the A4169 bypass. This key village was the base chosen by Abraham Darby III for his main factory. It has abundant water supplies provided by several streams which could be easily damned and harnessed to power machinery.

Originally from a Quaker family, Abraham Darby IV, as part of his conversion to Anglicanism, instigated and paid for the construction of Holy Trinity Church in Coalbrookdale in 1849, with his wife Matilda laying the foundation stone in 1851.

Coalbrookdale village scene – present day

Above: *Coalbrookdale Company Works – now housing the Ironbridge Gorge Museum Trust*

Below: *Coalbrookdale memorial, Paradise, Wellington Road, Ironbridge*

Construction was completed in 1854 and it was consecrated by the Bishop of Hereford.

The church was to play its part in the Great War as many village men served and a privileged few lie buried in its graveyard. Interior plaques commemorate all of the war dead and their service to the village. The main war memorial attached to the church is located outside the old Institute, at the junction of Wellington Road and Paradise, a few hundred yards down the road towards Ironbridge.

Coalport village

Nowadays, this quiet, extensively wooded hamlet runs parallel to the river on its north-eastern bank, about half a mile from the centre of Ironbridge, along the Lloyds and Coalport High Street, with the majority of the inhabitants' houses located on either side of the main throughroad. No longer a hub of industry, it is still home to the Coalport China Museum.

Coalport village, present day

Coalport China works museum featuring bottle kiln

Surprisingly, it was destined to rival Ironbridge in fame as a manufacturing town with the arrival of the Shropshire Canal in 1793 instigated by William Reynolds, whose father was the partner of Abraham Darby III the Iron Bridge builder.

Coalport also became the centre of one of the leading porcelain manufacturers of Britain with the classic chinaware of the Coalport China Company fired in their famous and innovative bottle kilns.

The Wedgwood factory, based at Burslem, Stoke-on-Trent, took interest and in 1934 absorbed Coalport China into their own business.

Jackfield village

Located on the south-western bank of the Severn, directly opposite Coalport across the river, Jackfield village centre is now sparse. It comprises cottages dotted along the riverbank road leading to St Mary the Virgin Church containing its memorial plaque to the Great War, and the village hall. A small tin chapel that was there

Jackfield village – present day

has now been moved to Blists Hill Museum. It is home to the Maw & Co and Craven Dunnill encaustic tile & ceramics factories. Both have long ceased trading in the town at the site of the old factories, which are now preserved as museums, being considered industrial heritage sites of national importance. It is also home to a famous brass band that can trace its history back to the turn of the twentieth century. A First World War memorial footbridge, opened in 1922, links Jackfield to Coalport.

Madeley village

This satellite to Ironbridge is located on the same side of the river above it on the plain overlooking the gorge with the Severn running through it. It was originally a mining village with several pits owned and run by the Anstice family.

Madeley has been the scene of some tragic coal mining disasters: one in 1864 involving the death of nine local colliers, and another in 1912 in which seven miners died including two children aged 14.

The decline in the coal industry in the first half of the twentieth century is reflected in the decline of Madeley's civic power and influence locally. It has latterly reverted to a district of the greater town of Telford.

St Michael's Church, in the older part of the original village, was to serve as the graveyard of many of Ironbridge's Great War dead.

Major Charles Allix Lavington Yate, the area's only Great War VC winner, lived in Madeley. This hero is commemorated on a plaque in St Michael's Church, and also on the memorial sepulchre in the main square which is inscribed with the dead of both world wars. There is a separate stone paving memorial plaque for Lavington Yate, which was laid in August 2016 and features in chapter six of this book.

St Michael's Church, Madeley

Lavington Yate Memorial plaque in St Michael's Church, Madeley

The *Wellington Journal and Shrewsbury News*

To give the reader a flavour of the Ironbridge area's social history in the lead-up and early months of the war we have included some snippets of daily life revealed through the pages of the only newspaper available. Ironbridge's own newspaper folded in the 1870s and the job of keeping its denizens informed and updated fell to the nearest weekly publication, the *Wellington Journal and Shrewsbury News*. With offices four miles away in the town centre of Wellington, established in 1854 by Thomas Leake, it took over the rival *Shropshire News* in 1874, and was to steadfastly report all the war news to the inhabitants for the duration and beyond. It was absorbed by the Shropshire Star Newspaper group and ceased publication in the 1960s.

Ironbridge area news round-up, 1914

Ironbridge town was judicially autonomous. It had its own 'Petty
Sessions' (minor criminal court), presided over most times by an
alderman/magistrate dispensing justice. In 1914 this was Mr A.B.
Dyas, who had also served as mayor. There was a similar judicial
set-up for the Madeley area. The *Journal* of 4 July 1914 reported
the following from the Ironbridge Petty Sessions:

Iron-Bridge
Assault *– Edward Garbett, labourer, Broseley was charged
with beating Edith Rogers and also with assaulting her baby,
Ada. She lived three doors down from the defendant.*

*About six in the evening when she was standing near her
house door with the baby in her arms, who was six months
old, defendant came out of his house and without any
provocation struck her once on the breast and twice on the
back, with his fist.*

*He also hit the baby with his open hand in the eye and left
a mark. She was unconscious for some moments – Defendant
stated that a bother arose over the children and when Mrs Rogers
called him names he struck her with open hand on the back and
if he struck the child it was an accident. On the first count he
was fined 15 shillings, including costs for beating the woman
and the other charge was dismissed.*

The *Journal* edition dated 19 September 1914 reports from the
Petty Sessions:

Iron-Bridge
Monday – Before Mr W. Roberts
   *Remanded – Richard Williams a well known Iron-Bridge
labourer was brought up in custody charged with stealing four
sacks and a quantity of barley, to the value of 14s 8d [74p],
the property of Harry Owen, maltster of Iron-Bridge - Sergeant
Morris proved the arrest and on his application, defendant was
remanded in custody until the Iron-Bridge Petty Sessions.*

Journal edition dated 14 November 1914 at the Madeley Petty Sessions reports:

Wounding at Madeley

George Parker (73) Labourer, Madeley, was charged with maliciously wounding Fredk Austin of Madeley. Mr Graham prosecuted and the defendant, who pleaded not guilty, conducted his own defence. Evidence on the behalf of the prosecution was to the effect that on the night of October 24th Austin was standing outside the Miners Arms[1] at Madeley when Parker struck him in the stomach with a pen-knife, causing a serious wound. Early in the evening Parker was in the public-house and during a conversation about a pipe with a customer named Aaron Lowe, prisoner said he had a good pipe once but a man named Groves struck him in a bother and broke it. He went on to say:

"I will have my revenge on him, I cannot forget and if I can see him I will disembowel him." After the incident P.C. Sargent, visited prisoner's lodgings and in answer to his knock Parker appeared at the door with a chopper in his hand. He was asked what he was doing with it and replied: "I thought it was someone else." The penknife was subsequently found behind a pantry door at Parker's lodgings – In reply to the prisoner, Austin denied that he struck him first – Giving evidence Parker said that on the day referred to he was having a "Birthday". He commenced drinking in the morning and altogether he spent about 3s & 6d in beer during the day. In the evening he visited the Miners Arms and subsequently while standing outside the inn, Austin who had also been in the house, struck him and kicked him in the stomach – In cross-examination Parker said that he was under the influence of drink and he could not recall having stabbed Austin but as there was no one else about at the time he must have done it. He had had no quarrel with him – Prisoner was found guilty.

How news of the Great War reached the Ironbridge area

The long hot summer of 1914 proved a pleasant diversion in Ironbridge and its denizens were busy enjoying every available

---

1   The Miners Arms exists today in Madeley at 74, Prince Street

entertainment, including regattas, coracle races on the Severn, and gaily-painted stalls in Ironbridge square's market which was carried over from the usual Friday due to the extended bank holiday period. Their thoughts were a million miles away from the events unfolding in Europe.

Surprisingly, news of the war's outbreak was considered a low-key affair at the time and was relegated to page 7 of the *Wellington Journal* in the issue dated 8 August 1914 and not in the front page banner headlines. The people of the UK initially considered this foreign conflict as a storm in a teacup. It was only later that people suspected hostilities might escalate and affect their lives beyond a minor inconvenience and a shift in topical gossip over the breakfast table. The public response, fuelled by lurid press reports of German atrocities in Belgium, was a mixture of naivety based partly on *Boy's Own* adventure books and patriotic zeal.

The recruitment and enlistment of the men of Ironbridge
Most of the Ironbridge area's eligible men read or heard about the war's declaration either by word of mouth, from handbills, or from the mass recruitment campaign conducted through the pages of the *Wellington Journal*.

The British army was woefully under strength at the outbreak, comprising volunteers and career servicemen numbering just over 83,000 with 247,000 in reserve.

So there began an immediate enlistment campaign targeting the UK's male civilian population between 18 and 45 years old. Recruitment posters and press appeals were produced by the government's War Office. Adverts were used depicting Lord Herbert Horatio Kitchener, Secretary of State for War in Herbert Asquith's wartime coalition government. The campaign worked so well it swelled the army's ranks by a half a million men within the first six months of the war. Young men, eager to prove their patriotism, were recruited at various special purpose enlistment offices hastily installed nationwide. They believed they would share a short holiday in France with their pals and return home unscathed and victorious by Christmas at the latest.

Old Library, Severn Bank, off the Wharfage, Ironbridge, present day

In Ironbridge, the eligible enlistees would mass in the square before marching to the Old Armoury and Drill Hall off the market square or the Old Library off the wharfage, and form an orderly queue.

Others were recruited to join local territorial army units. Territorial battalions were originally only pledged to fight domestically in defence of the realm. Most battalions were to forego this and send contingents abroad.

Based in most recruiting offices across the land were the company sergeants of the local regiments – in this case the predominant regiment of Shropshire, the King's Shropshire Light Infantry (KSLI). This prestigious regiment dominates the Great War casualty lists in the area, and also has its own shrine at the National Memorial Arboretum in Alrewas, Staffordshire.

Once enlisted, recruits 'taking the king's shilling', as army service was dubbed, underwent initial training for six weeks before being assigned to one of the many KSLI battalions. Some men joined other regiments, usually if they were away from home on detachment from local factories or perhaps studying for an apprenticeship. Others joined other branches of the armed services, not just land-based but maritime and latterly airborne, as we shall discover in the various accounts, many of which are revealed in this book for the first time.

Kitchener's poster depiction was to adorn public places such as libraries town halls, sports grounds, music halls and of course recruitment offices. The response helped amass the largest army of citizen soldiery the country had ever witnessed. By June 1915 his campaign had attracted 2.6 million extra men to join the Expeditionary Force. Over the course of the war hundreds of thousands more were to answer this call.

These volunteers, dubbed 'Kitchener's Army', comprised 'Pals' battalions made up of townships and factory workforces who mustered groups of men from their local areas and communities. They were encouraged to enlist together and were allowed to keep together where possible when drafted into their regiments.

War recruitment news, Ironbridge area, circa 1914

The *Wellington Journal* was keen to report on the progress of recruitment locally. The edition dated 8 August 1914 reported direct from Ironbridge:

The Town on Wednesday [5th] morning presented quite an animated appearance on the occasion of the local Territorials awaiting orders in the market square to entrain.

The streets were thronged with people discussing the war. Within a short period nearly 40 recruits were enrolled. A great multitude assembled on the old bridge and its approaches and cheered the men as they marched to the railway station and as the train steamed out of the town for Shrewsbury shouts of 'Good Luck' rent the air while women and girls wept... The Rev. C.B. Crowe (Coalbrookdale) appropriately addressed the Territorials before they left the town. Mr J.W. White and other ambulance men have also volunteered for the front.

Edition dated 17 October 1914 reported the mobilisation of Ironbridge troops:

> ***A good Welcome*** *– Some hundreds of people lined the old iron bridge on Wednesday night [14th] and gave the 110 members of the D (Ironbridge) company of Territorials who had volunteered for foreign service a most enthusiastic welcome on their return from Kent. These men were in excellent spirits at having been selected for duty in India.*

Edition dated 24 October 1914 reported further mobilisations:

> ***Iron-Bridge*** *– Some thousands of people hailing from all parts of the district on Saturday [17th] gave a hearty send-off to the Iron-bridge Territorials who have volunteered for service abroad. The Madeley & Coalbrookdale combined bands played patriotic marches through the streets and appropriate selections at the railway station which was crowded with spectators. Jackfield Band was also present and played suitable music. After the combined bands had played, the Territorials rent the air with the popular refrain: 'My Sweetheart till I die' – As the train steamed out of the station the band played the National Anthem and the huge crowd shouted themselves hoarse. The Rev. A.E. Shields (rector) was present and shook hands with all the soldiers giving them words of encouragement...*

The same report dated 24 October marks the arrival of war refugees to the town:

> ***Belgian Refugees*** *– A family of Belgian Refugees had a hearty reception in the town on Monday evening [19th]. The Rev. C.B. Crowe (vicar) accompanied them from Birmingham and they were received at the Dale Station by Mr. Rawdon Smith, Mr H. Hughes; Miss Doughty & Miss Fox-Davies. They were taken to their new home, the late Unionist Club,*

which had been furnished by the church people and others of Coalbrookdale and is very comfortable. The refugees came direct from Antwerp...

Local factories' participation in the Great War

Leading up to the war it would seem that some local firms did not always enjoy harmonious relationships with their various workforces, particularly in Coalport. The *Journal* dated 1 August 1914 reports a strike in progress:

> **Coalport: The Strike** – *There is a dispute with the Coalport China Company and 26 of their decorators who have been on strike a fortnight... A meeting was held on Wednesday night in Ironbridge market place conducted under the auspices of the Amalgamated Society of male & female Pottery Workers...*
>
> *Mr J. Booth (Stoke-on-Trent secretary) stated at the meeting that he was told that there was a real need for some dispute to happen here as the employers did not pay too much in wages. All that the trade union desired was a living wage, and he did not think that anyone ought to object to that...*
>
> *The trade in question was a skilled one and some of the work in pottery was often disastrous to life and health, for instance the lead process – and yet these men were only paid a paltry sum for their work. Was it too much to ask to be allowed to live? This was the second week of the strike and the employers still refused to discuss the matter with a trade union representative. He thought it was time the people at Coalport should be 'making things hum a bit'... It was time they asserted their union rights & that could only be done by combining... It was a scandalous state of affairs that such wages should be paid in Coalport.*

After the war's declaration (particularly in war-related industries) strikes were banned by order of the provisions of DORA (the Defence of the Realm Act, 1914). The UK's businesses, especially those directly contracted to the war effort (such as the railway companies) were obliged to support the war and it was felt the rest of industry should comply with positive patriotic action. Besides, compliance offered boundless lucrative opportunities to those in the position to supply raw or finished materials and goods for the war effort. From 1916 onwards every square inch of factory space across the land was turned over to war production. The bigger companies in the Ironbridge area responded to the nation's call to arms in their various ways, some with munitions component manufacturing, as in the case of the Coalbrookdale Company (Abraham Darby). For other businesses in the gorge the best way to demonstrate loyalty was to contribute with the only other asset they had – their workforce. The famous Maw & Co and Craven Dunnill factories at Jackfield raised their own 'pals battalion' comprising men from their own workforce and this was deemed as a patriotic duty by the management.

The Maws factory/Craven Dunnill in the war

The company of Maw & Co (which still exists today in a truncated form in Stoke-on-Trent and is now owned by its one-time rival Craven Dunnill) was founded in the 1850s by George and Arthur Maw at a factory in Worcester, taking over the failed Worcester Tileries company. This venture was funded by their father John Hornby Maw, the great Scottish surgical instrument maker whose main claim to fame was that he was the inventor of the baby-feeding bottle. After recognising his sons' design skills he agreed to set them up in business. They were briefly located at Broseley before moving to the Benthall works which nowadays is the site of the Maws craft centre.

Today's visitors to the centre approach the site through the original factory's magnificent cast-iron western gate. Through these gates passed two million pieces of product by 1882 making it one of the most prolific tile manufacturers the UK has ever seen. These encaustic ceramic tile products once graced many an official building both civic and public across the whole of the world (some still decorate local buildings in the town, such as the Best Western Valley Hotel).

Maws factory now craft centre, Jackfield, near Ironbridge, modern day

In the main ground floor hallway of the old administration block (now subdivided into private apartments) opposite the staircase sits a series of three commemoration plaques made out of Maw & Co's own tile product affixed to the wall, commissioned in the early 1920s to commemorate their factory war dead. They are subdivided into one main and two side tablets some five feet high and about ten feet wide. They contain an alphabetical list of the names of all the Maws local factory and area volunteers who formed a pals company and went off to fight the war, never to return.

Another local world-renowned tile company was located in the Gorge: Craven Dunnill, which still exists in a smaller form today. We shall later discover the Great War history of one of their employees, William Harry Stephan, told for the first time in this book.

Maws main block vestibule, plaque of ceramic tiles, created as a First World War memorial

Personal accounts: Ironbridge servicemen in the War
The Reynolds family of Jackfield

In 1914 Mrs Nellie Reynolds lived at 252, Werps Road,[2] with her husband and son. She was destined to lose both to the Great War. Her son was killed at the Somme in 1916 and her husband was to follow when he died two years after the war's end from 'war effects' (the semi-official term for poisoning by chemical warfare (gas)). The Wrekin Honour Roll listings briefly state:

> *28458 Sergeant Arthur REYNOLDS, The Depot, The King's (Liverpool Regiment). Husband of Mrs. Nellie Reynolds, 252 Werps Road, Jackfield. Died at home from 'war effects' 3rd November 1920. Buried at Broseley Churchyard.*

---

2   *Werps Road was destined to be wiped from the map in the 1952 Tuckies and Jackfield landslide*

31122 Lance Corporal George REYNOLDS, 6th Battalion, South Staffordshire Regiment. Husband of Mrs A. Reynolds, 252 Werps Road, Jackfield. Killed in action at Regina Trench, Thiepval, France, 21st October 1916. (Son of Sergeant Arthur Reynolds)

(George is listed on the Coalport/Jackfield memorial bridge plaque)

The story of William Harry Stephan (Craven Dunnill employee)

The following is the story of one of Craven Dunnill's employees in the Great War and his friend and fellow enlistee at the time, both locals – as told to me by a local inhabitant – Ronald Miles of Jackfield:

> *My relative William Stephan lived on the Lloyds and at the time of the Great War was apprenticed to the Craven Dunnill factory group just up the river from the Maws factory. He was working away for them up in Preston, near Manchester when one day, he was accosted in the street by two young women who demanded to know why he wasn't in uniform... My maternal Uncle William Harry Stephan is mentioned on the Coalport and Jackfield war memorial footbridge plate and inside Jackfield church monuments.[3]*

It was customary at the time for roaming bands of females and other self-appointed groups to hand out white feathers in public places. Deemed as a mark of cowardice this practice was not discouraged by the government who had just issued the Defence of the Realm Act. These unprecedented regulations imposed strict codes of behaviour on the populace, particularly civilians, during wartime. Part of its intention was to combat domestic espionage and control the movement of foreign nationals within UK borders.

---

3   see chapter 6: Jackfield St Mary the Virgin Church monument

A memorial tile was placed by his mother in the village's place of worship, the Tin (corrugated iron) Chapel. It was later donated to Blists Hill Museum, a local living history museum located in the Severn Valley Gorge near Coalport village. Stephan is a Huguenot name. The Huguenot forebears of the Stephan family came up the river to Jackfield, Coalport and Ironbridge during the late eighteenth century.

The Huguenots' association with Ironbridge

France has always been essentially a catholic country and during the eighteenth century this came to bear oppressively on other religious groups. The 1652 Edict of Nantes allowing freedom of worship across France was overturned by Louis XIV thereby compromising the Huguenots. This Calvinist Protestant brotherhood of families, based in central and south-western France, were persecuted. Some were to leave their homes forever. Comprising mainly artisans with manufacturing trade skills, some fifty thousand Huguenots migrated to Britain. Settling first in London, twenty-five thousand later spread out across the country. The Stephans eventually resettled in the Ironbridge area. Drawn there by the burgeoning diverse manufacturing revolution headed by the Abraham Darby company they found that their skills were in high demand.

Ron Miles: *This is where our family connection to the Huguenots begins, as the name of Stephan derives from this previous bloodline.*

Across the river three unrelated soldiers called the 'Ironbridge Stephans' were all engineers involved in making war weaponry. Some young women of Ironbridge also sent them white feathers because they weren't in uniform.

This tactic of public humiliation certainly worked with William Stephan who seemed to be so affected by this challenge to his manhood from total strangers that he joined a local army force in 1916 – the Loyal North Lancashire regiment.

His death is recorded in the Wrekin Roll of Honour entry and reads,

*36893 **Private William Harry Stephan** 1/4 Battalion The Loyal North Lancashire Regiment, Born and lived at Jackfield, Killed in action in Flanders, 18th July 1917*

It is not known which action he died in but it was part of the Passchendaele campaign. The fighting was intense in this corner of France during that period. Some clue is given in the military actions for the 1/4th Battalion, recalled in the following regimental diary extract from the *Great War History*:

Loyal North Lancs
***1/4th Battalion Territorial Force*[4]**
04.05.1915 *Mobilised for war and landed at Boulogne where the formation became 154th Brigade of the 51st Division and engaged in various actions on the Western Front including; The Battle of Festubert, The Second Action of Givenchy.*

During 1917: The Battle of Pilckem Ridge & The Battle of Menin Road Ridge.

William 'Harry' Stephan was involved in one of these later actions of July-September 1917 and lost his life fighting in this bloody offensive as part of the Passchendaele campaign which ranks second only to the Somme as the bloodiest battle in the war (see chapter 4).

William Stephan's Great War diary extract

For the duration of the war William maintained his own rough diary:

Joined the army on Tuesday, February 27th 1917... was inspected by Sir John French on Tuesday 24th April... Arrived Boulogne Wednesday 23rd May... came under fire for the first time on Monday 2nd July... two planes downed Saturday 7th July... Midnight shelled – came in support Sunday 8th July.

The final poignantly enigmatic note for Sunday, 15 July, just has two words: *Front line.* After Stephan was killed by a sniper's bullet on 18 July, the diary was found by a friend and colleague from his unit (who was later killed) and subsequently returned to the family.

---

4   meaning originally raised to be home-based but volunteered for overseas service

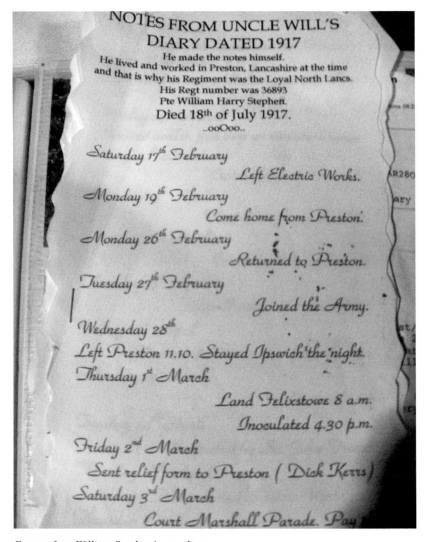

Extract from William Stephan's war diary

The story of Edward Colley in the War

Ron Miles resumes his narrative to tell us more about Edward Colley, Harry's friend and neighbour who lived on the Lloyds at Coalford and joined up about the same time:

> *Mrs Colley and Mrs Stephan my grandmother lived on the*
> *Lloyds, Jackfield, and knew everyone so we must presume*

both Edward and Harry played and grew up together, on the same street. Mrs Colley lost her son Edward who is mentioned on the Jackfield memorial bridge as well as the Ironbridge memorial amongst a total of 44 names and is maintained by the local branch of the British Legion.

The Wrekin Roll of Honour entry for Private Colley is unusually brief and reads:

16642 Private Edward Colley, 8th Battalion KSLI
Son of Mr Walter Colley, 48 Coalford Jackfield
Killed in action in Salonika 18th September 1918

Edward Colley's battalion was to see much distinguished service in many other theatres of war across Europe and the middle east as recorded in the 8th Battalion KSLI Battle Honours First World War: *Mons; Aisne 1914, 1918; Ypres 1914, 1917, 1918; Somme 1916, 1918; Lys; Hindenburg Line; Suvla; Gaza; Baghdad; Kilimanjaro. Retreat from Mons; Marne 1914, 1918; Langemarck 1914; Gheluvelt; Nonne Bosschen; Givenchy 1914; Aubers; Festubert 1915; Loos; Albert 1916; Bazentin; Pozières; Guillemont; Ginchy; Fleurs-Courcelette; Morval; Ancre Heights; Ancre 1916; Arras 1917, 1918; Scarpe 1917; Arleux; Messines 1917; Pilckem; Menin Road; Polygon Wood; Poelcappelle; Passchendaele; Cambrai 1917, 1918; St Quentin; Bapaume 1918; Estaires; Bailleul; Kemmel; Béthune; Scherpenberg; Soissonnais-Ourcq; Drocourt-Quéant; Épehy; Canal du Nord; St Quentin Canal; Courtrai; Selle; Sambre; France and Flanders 1914-18; Doiran 1917; Macedonia 1917; Sari Bair; Gallipoli 1915; Egypt 1916; Nebi Samwil; Jerusalem; Jaffa; Tell Asur; Palestine 1917-18; Tigris 1916; Kut al Amara 1917; Mesopotamia 1916-18; East Africa 1914-16.*

The Salonika Campaign (1915-18)
Edward Colley's brief war service was as a combatant in an Allied campaign in Salonika. It is doubtful if any of the men of Ironbridge, including Colley, had ever heard of this place before to the war. However this operation was deemed to be vital to the success of a

broader war being fought against Germany and her allies beyond the Western Front. At the time of the war, the Greek port known as Salonika (now called Thessaloniki) on the North Aegean coast, was central to an Allied campaign to assist Serbia and to undermine Bulgaria who had allied itself with Germany. This campaign was really just an extension of the Balkan Wars being fought in the run-up to the war.

The *Wellington Journal* was keen to keep its readers abreast of the situation with this report from the edition dated 19 February 1916, page 7, under 'War News':

> **'At Salonika**
>
> *'It was reported from Athens that conversations were proceeding between Greece and Rumania with a view to a closer union in the prosecution of their common interests.*
>
> *According to a Rome message Rumania has contracted for the purchase of 14,000 horses in Russia. It was reported that Bulgaria had demanded the transport of 180 waggon loads of food through Rumania. It was stated that before the end of March 50,000 Serbians once more thoroughly fit for active service would be sent from Corfu to reinforce the Allied Army at Salonika.*
>
> *A report from Salonika said that the Greek cavalry brigade was leaving there, owing to the difficulty obtaining supplies.'*

From the flavour of the article we can see that the Bulgarians had seen which way the political wind was blowing as they had participated in oppressing the Balkan states for many years in a bid to dominate the region of Asia Minor (including Turkey) and the Greek peninsula. With minor skirmishes occurring, referred to as wars, on Bulgaria's borders for many years, the opportunity arose to align itself with Germany and thereby consolidate its stranglehold on this strategically important region, buffered as it was in south-eastern Europe with Serbia and Macedonia on its western border, Greece to the South, and Turkey and Russia to the east across the Black Sea.

In 1915 France and Britain thought that a Balkan strategy was a way of alleviating the deadlock on the western front by forcing Germany to rethink its campaign in this area. This would weaken their forces on the Western and Eastern fronts as they would be obliged to commit more forces to uphold their position. The armies of several countries comprising Britain's Expeditionary Force (which included Edward Colley's 8th Battalion KSLI), Serbia and Romania, as well as Italy, were combined to bear down on Bulgaria. A late campaign, commenced in September of 1918, under Allied commander Franchet d'Espèrey, saw the last remnants of the Bulgarian forces rapidly collapse. It is estimated that over 600,000 Allied troops were committed to the Salonika campaign. Private Edward Colley of Ironbridge was one of the battle statistics. Colley's family, who lived at Lloyds Head, could afford to have their own memorial plaque made by the ceramic tile factory at Craven Dunnill (the same factory as William Stephan's).

Other Ironbridge-area casualties in the Salonika campaign

WR/207074 Sapper John BOWEN, Royal Engineers, Born at Jackfield.
Died at Salonika, 6 September 1918.

21069 Private Horatio Ellis EVANS, 7th Battalion South Wales Borderers.
Eldest son of Horatio William Evans, The Lloyds, Ironbridge.
Killed in Action in Salonika, 17 September 1918. Age 32.

The Ironbridge-area rail link and the war

The railways arrived late in this part of the world (circa 1856) due to land disputes. Ironbridge enjoyed its own link called the Dale station, located opposite the bridge on the far bank from the town. Being part of the GWR, it had its own hotel accommodation alongside the track – the Station Hotel. This was a stopover en route to the fleshpots of Shrewsbury and the coastal route to Wales and Aberystwyth. At the time of the Great War it was run

Postcard depicting Ironbridge Dale Station, circa 1906

by Mr and Mrs Burton, who had two sons of war-service eligible age. Although helping their parents to run the business they both felt compelled to enlist, which they did with their parents' blessing. Disaster was to strike when they lost both sons in the same year, as the Wrekin District Roll of Honour records:

> *45259 Private Harry BURTON – Royal Defence Corps. Son of Mrs E. Burton, Station Hotel, Ironbridge. Died at Military Hospital Oswestry, 4th July 1917. Buried at Broseley Cemetery.*

> *30399 Private Reginald BURTON, 1st Battalion, King's Own Royal Lancaster Regiment. Son of Mr E. Burton, Station Hotel, Ironbridge; brother to Harry, Killed in action in Flanders, 12th October 1917. Commemorated on Tyne Cot Memorial, Passchendaele, Belgium. Age 35.*

The Station Hotel still stands today and is a bar/restaurant in private ownership.

The Station Hotel, Ironbridge, modern day

Coalbrookdale rail link
The branch-line station at Coalbrookdale was to suffer tragedy when Mr Marshall the Stationmaster lost his only son to the Great War. Corporal Herbert Marshall was a casualty of the Gallipoli campaign and his details are covered in chapter 2.

Rail transport of troops and equipment to the front
At the very beginning of the war the government made provision to effectively nationalise the whole of the UK railway system. Company owners were informed that they were to operate under strict war office timetables and fixed contracts were to be kept in force for the duration. This measure was to cause several post-war bankruptcies, as rail companies found their books refused to balance in the face of rising costs. Freight and passenger charges could not be increased during the war years to cover maintenance and upgrades to worn out rolling stock due to this draconian legislation. The burden of using adapted rolling stock to transport

horses and war equipment coupled to the frequency of line usage meant spiralling costs to operators.

Opening battles and early defeats (1914-15)
When the BEF's embarkation to France began on 9 August 1914 it numbered some 80,000 men. Once fully mustered at their concentration point at Maubeuge on the 20th, they were deployed with the French 2nd and 5th Armies to support their attack on the Aisne and the Meuse at the town of Mons, which is located on the French/Belgian border. The BEF's early campaigns were destined not to be as successful as hoped, when it was realised they were up against a formidable enemy in the shape of the German army whose superior forces were well prepared and waiting for battle.

Battle of Mons, 23 August 1914
The Battle of Mons was the first major action of the BEF in the conflict. It was a subsidiary action to the battle of the frontiers in which the Allies clashed with the Bosch on the French borders. At Mons the BEF attempted to hold the line of the Mons-Condé canal against the advancing German First Army. Although the British fought well and inflicted disproportionate casualties on the enemy, they were eventually forced to retreat. This was due both to the greater strength of the Germans and the sudden retreat of the French Fifth Army which exposed the British right flank. After a bloody skirmish lasting several weeks the British and French armies were forced to retreat and take up defensive positions at Le Cateau en Cambrésis.

Battle of Le Cateau, 26 August 1914
Whereas the battle of Mons had been an infantryman's fight, the battle at Le Cateau was an artilleryman's. It was essentially a rearguard action to try to stem the German advance after the Allies' chaotic retreat from Mons. The British were dug in to the north-west of the Wadelles river on unsuitable boggy and uneven country. The BEF artillery were deployed some 250 yards behind the infantry line in open formation. Due to the concealed offset German artillery

positions they became a target alongside their infantry and were consequently heavily pounded resulting in a great many casualties.

This key engagement is where the Ironbridge area was to win its first major war decoration with the courageous rearguard action of a Madeley man – Major C. Lavington Yate who was awarded the VC posthumously.

The Battle of the Marne, 5-12 September 1914

As the French 5th Army and the BEF retreated, the German Schlieffen Plan began to unravel. The plan contained several inherent flaws and, as the French and the BEF retreated, the German 1st and 2nd armies were drawn to the south and the east, instead of turning to the west as planned. This resulted in the 1st Army passing to the East of Paris. The French commander, Joffre, saw a major opportunity to halt the German advance as the German 1st Army was found to be vulnerable to an attack in its flank from the direction of Paris in the west. The French 6th Army began its advance against the Germans in September, beginning with the Battle of the Marne.

This is arguably the most important battle of the War. By its end, the Germans had begun a general withdrawal along a 250-mile front and the Schlieffen Plan was dead.

The Battle of the Aisne, 12-15 September 1914

The German retreat ended along the line of the River Aisne. Their forces dug in along the heights of the Chemin de Dames, north of the river, and created a system of trenches protected by belts of barbed wire and defended by machine guns and artillery. The trench line soon extended south 600 km to the Swiss frontier.

This seeming retreat had resulted in a wave of Allied optimism and some senior commanders had envisaged driving the Germans back to their borders. However, in a series of costly attacks over two weeks, known as the Battle of the Aisne, the French and British failed to penetrate the German defences. Trench warfare had begun and the deadlock which resulted was not to be broken until the spring of 1918.

War news: Madeley serviceman, Lavington Yate VC award

These initial battles and early engagements led to some courageous exploits along the Western Front including awards won by the men of the Ironbridge area. One of the earliest was the VC that was won at Le Cateau by Major Charles Allix Lavington Yate, known as 'Cal' to his friends, a pet name devolved from his first three initials. This hero of the Great War was a career officer and the outbreak found him serving in the 2nd Battalion, King's Own Yorkshire Light Infantry. Born to the vicar of St Michael's Church, Madeley, on 14 March 1872, he was Sandhurst officer-trained and served with distinction, rising to the rank of major. He was also fairly high-ranking in social terms, his cousin Sir Charles Yate being the 1st baronet.

On the day of the engagement at Le Cateau, the 2nd Battalion King's Own Yorkshire Light Infantry along with Major Lavington Yate were told to stock up their trenches with ammunition and supplies and to expect a lengthy fight.

Their valiant rearguard action belies the tragic outcome which is described in the Wrekin Roll of Honour:

> *LN/89506 Major Charles Allix Lavington Yate, VC, 2nd Battalion, The King's Own (Yorkshire Light Infantry), Son of the late Vicar of Madeley. Died from wounds while a prisoner of war in German hands 20th September 1914. Joined the army in 1892, promoted to Captain in 1899 and to Major in 1902.*
>
> *Saw active service with the Tirah Expeditionary Force, in the South African War and the Russo-Japanese War. Aged 42. The citation for his Victoria Cross reads: 'Commanded one of the two companies that remained to the end in the Trenches at Le Cateau on 25th August 1914. When all the officers were killed or wounded and all ammunition exhausted, he led his 19 survivors against the enemy in a charge in which he was severely wounded, then picked up by the enemy. He died from his wounds, while in POW captivity, less than a month later.*

*Major Charles Allix
Lavington Yate,
VC as PoW.*

Of the four other VCs won that day at Le Cateau, one of them,
Lance Corporal Frederick Holmes, said of him, 'Had he lived he
would have become a general – he was always in front of his men
and his constant cry was, "Follow me, lads".'

War news: Ironbridge-area service personnel
The *Journal* of 2 November 1914 reports a local soldier's readiness
for war:

> **'Coalbrookdale: Letters home**
> *Sergt. W.A. Lloyd, A Company, 3rd Batt. K.S.L.I. A resident
> in Wellington Road **Coalbrookdale**, he is at present with his
> Company in South Wales. He writes that he has had 17 years
> with the Regiment, and is now working harder than at any
> other time he can remember, but they get plenty to eat and
> drink. The Sergeant who is an excellent Euphonium player,
> is with the band. For 12 years he has been a member of the
> Coalbrookdale Band.*
>
> *He is an enthusiastic footballer and was on the committee of
> the now-defunct Iron-Bridge FC.*

General war-related news: Ironbridge area 1914

The *Journal* of 14 November highlights concerns about local recruitment:

> *Letters to the Editor – (Dear Sir)*
> *Coalbrookdale*
> *I should like to refer to the criticism that is being made in respect to recruiting in Shropshire, and in justice to the patriotism of the people of Coalbrookdale, to say that Coalbrookdale has not only fulfilled the call of Earl Kitchener for three per cent of the population but has exceeded it by 1¾ per cent. It has sent 71 to the service out of the 307 houses; the works (Darby's – Dale Factory) has sent more than 100 out of a possible 500 workmen above 19 years; and I may add that there is one district containing 46 homes where there is not one single person left of eligible age. If all of the parishes of Shropshire will respond to the call as nobly as Coalbrookdale, there will be no need to detach the word proud from Salopia or to brand her sons with the stigma of unloyalty. Yours, John Barker*

The edition dated 5 December 1914 reports that the ladies of Ironbridge were doing their bit for the war effort:

> *Iron-Bridge*
> *For The Soldiers – The members of the Wesley Guild have for the last few weeks been busy making articles for our soldiers at the front and this week a large parcel has been despatched to them consisting of – 2 shirts, 15 mufflers, 24 pairs of mittens, 13 pairs of socks, 5 helmets and 5 body belts.*

CHAPTER 2

1915: The Common Clay

The first Great War telegraph sent to British forces read:
**'Admiralty to all ships: immediate: Engage German ships
and commence fighting.'**
*(Issued by Winston Churchill, 1st Sea Lord of the Admiralty,
11:15 pm, 4 August 1914)*

Allied progress in the War - faltering beginnings

By early 1915 stalemate had prevailed over the Western Front for months and the public were clamouring for military success. The UK government sought good news from any quarter to justify what was turning out to be an expensive and prolonged disaster in terms of material resources as well as the nation's lifeblood. Appalling casualty figures were now being collated for all the opening battles. Even the first Allied success at Ypres in late 1914 had been very costly, resulting in the mass build-up of forces on both sides. For the first time on European soil, vast armies piled up behind trenches nose to nose across sometimes only metres of open ground. In early 1915 it was realised by the Allies that hopes of a short sharp war were rapidly fading into the distance to be replaced by a long-drawn-out affair committing huge resources of manpower and materials.

Trench warfare – the new/old practice

As numbers grew on both sides the weight of engagements and resultant stalemates forced them to consolidate territorial gains. This could only be done by the use of an ancient but effective tactic – the trench. Both sides would naturally let their respective infantry dig in for the night to recuperate from the day's fighting. These were initially crude structures involving men scraping holes in the ground to escape enemy shellfire and rifle fusillades as well as the elements. However, the overwhelming need to rest and cook a simple meal was the main priority in most infantrymen's minds. As fronts became more static, trenches became more permanent. It was soon realised that as a means of defending a long front and resisting the dreaded counter-attack, trenches could be lightly manned, well-fortified and easily reinforced to quell any skirmish breaches or full-scale counter-attacks.

These 'temporary respite shelters' became very elaborate structures, virtually underground cities, often self-contained and fully-powered, comprising many subterranean levels each with intricate defences. They were also the starting points for vast tunnel constructions extended under enemy-held territory, used to secrete huge explosive mines in stockpile.

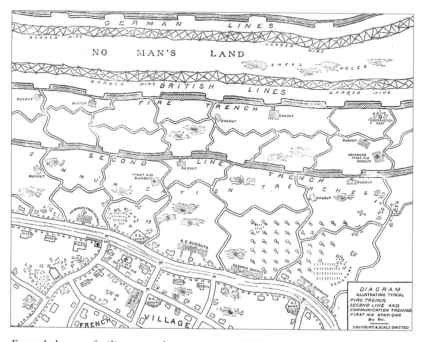

Example layout of military trench systems, circa 1915

Local Heroes: The Darby family and the Great War

The company that built the famous Iron Bridge had expanded from the little business making cooking pots founded by the first Abraham Darby by his son Abraham III and devolved into the Coalbrookdale Company. By the time of the Great War Alfred Darby was the senior patriarch of the family, holding the chairmanship of the company. The family seat, having been at Madeley Court, was now at Adcote House, Little Ness, Shropshire, built for them by the Scottish architect Richard Norman Shaw RA. Maurice Darby, Alfred's only son, was also the nephew of Sir George Arthur, also of Adcote.

Maurice Darby (1894-1915) – his part in the Great War

Maurice Alfred Alexander Darby was born on 6 May 6 1894 in Chelsea, the only son of Alfred E.W. and Frederica L.J. Darby, of Little Ness, Salop.

Besides being the last male heir of the famous Ironbridge dynasty he was also destined to become a Great War casualty.

He was killed in action at the Battle of Neuve Chapelle on 11 March 1915. He was 20 years old when he joined the Grenadier Guards in 1914. In October he went to France with the 7th Division

Lieutenant Maurice Darby (left) with unnamed army colleague

of the Expeditionary Force where he served in the trenches that winter. As with so many young men he seemed excited to go to war and do his patriotic duty. He was also brave enough to be 'mentioned in despatches', although the action is not specified. In January 1915, in an idle moment at his post at the front, he wrote on a few sheets of paper, 'One day in the Trenches', complaining he was too lazy to write a diary, but that one day he would have to do so.

Unlike tens of thousands of other soldiers who were buried where they fell on the battlefield, or nearby, his body came home. During massed battles the casualties tended to lie where they fell in the confusion of the fighting. After Maurice's body had lain on the battlefield for four days, his maternal uncle, General Sir George Arthur, found him. Despite great personal risk he eventually located and recovered the body. He then arranged for it to be brought home to Shropshire and buried at St Martin's church in Little Ness village.

The inscription on the grave of Maurice in St Martin's Little Ness reads,

St Martin's Church, Little Ness, Shropshire

In proud and loving memory of Maurice Darby whose body having lain for four days on the battlefield of Neuve Chapelle was, after a long night search in front of the enemy lines, recovered and brought home by his uncle George Arthur to be laid to rest on this spot.

Sir George Arthur (1860-1946) and the Great War

Sir George Compton Archibald Arthur was born in 1860, the son of Colonel Sir Frederick Arthur and Lady Elizabeth Hay-Drummond. He succeeded to the title of 3rd Baronet Arthur of Upper Canada on 1 June 1878. He later married Kate Hamet Brandon, on 11 August 1898.

Grave of Maurice Darby, Little Ness, Shropshire

Adcote Hall, Little Ness, Shropshire, home to Maurice Darby's family (nowadays Adcote School for Girls)

Gaining the rank of lieutenant in the service of the 2nd Life Guards he fought in both the Boer War and the First World War. In 1914-16 he held the office of personal private secretary to the Secretary of State for War, Lord Kitchener. On learning that his nephew Maurice was missing in 1915, he persuaded Kitchener, and by default the War Office, to let him mount the search and recovery operation personally from the active war zone around Neuve Chapelle. For obvious operational reasons this was normally not permitted. Similar requests from relatives of other fatalities, both military and civilian, were declined. But Arthur pulled rank and convinced them to ignore protocol and his actions were sanctioned. Among the reasons given was that Maurice was of noble family and was the last of the male line of the Darbys. Sir George was to spend four days searching among active battle sites braving constant enemy fire until, on the verge of abandoning his search, he finally found his poor dead nephew and secured the body from the open field where it lay. The chaos on the ground post-war made further recoveries impossible. Sir George Arthur went on to write a number of biographies including those of Kitchener and Earl Haig. He died at the age of 85 on 14 January 1946.

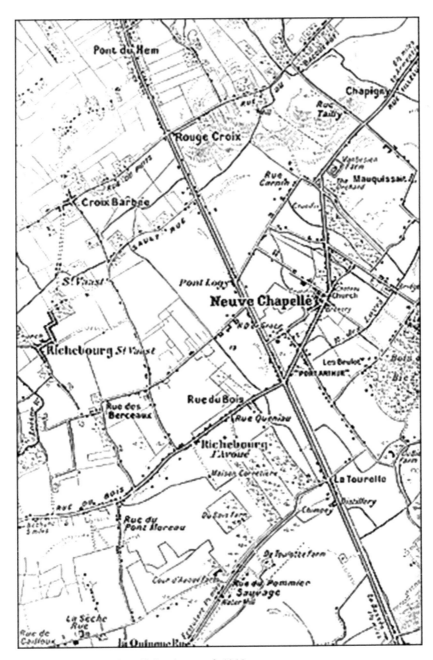

Diagram of Neuve Chapelle battleground, 1915

Battle of Neuve Chapelle, 10-12 March 1915

The Battle of Neuve Chapelle, in which Maurice Darby died, was fought over three days and represented an attempt to test the strength of the German lines by drawing out their resources. It was one of the first ever combined BEF and Allied offensives and was planned for 1915 in the Artois region of France. The Germans threatened the road, rail and canal junctions at La Bassée from the south. The First Army Division under the command of General Sir Douglas Haig attacked from the North making some headway. However the gains could not be consolidated as there was a lack of artillery to keep the enemy pinned down. The original plan was for the French Tenth Army to capture Vimy Ridge as well as the north end of the Artois plateau, from Lens to La Bassée. However the French part of the offensive was cancelled when the British were unable to relieve the French IX Corps which had been intended to move south for the French attack. Overall command and control was severely undermined at one point by equipment shortages. Communications between the infantry and artillery broke down when the telephone system failed. Early on 12 March the Germans launched a counter-attack, comprising twenty infantry battalions, which impeded the BEF assault.

Neuve Chapelle was a small-scale attack with modest objectives when compared with later battles. By the time the BEF assault was halted only one mile of terrain had been captured. Both the Germans and the BEF had suffered over 11,000 casualties. This near disaster fed naturally into the next Allied campaign, designated as Hill 60, which was fought south of the Ypres position.

The Battle for Hill 60 (Second Battle of Ypres), 17 April to 7 May

This key engagement followed on from the Neuve Chapelle operation and took place between 17 April and 7 May 1915, near Hill 60, south of Ypres on the Western Front. Hill 60 had been captured by the German 30th Division on 11 November 1914, during the First Battle of Ypres (19 October - 22 November 1914). Initial French preparations to raid the hill were continued by the British 28th Division, which took over the line in February 1915 and

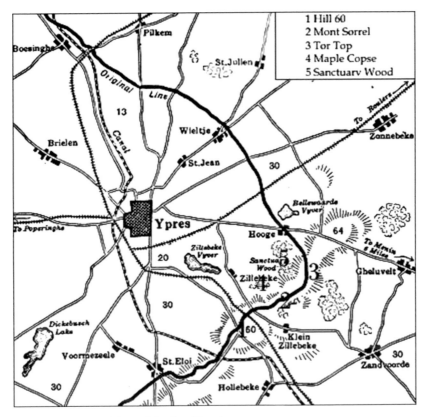

Location of Hill 60 (Second Battle of Ypres)

then by the 5th Division. The plan was expanded into an ambitious attempt to capture the hill, despite advice that Hill 60 could not be held unless the 'Caterpillar' nearby was also occupied. It was found that Hill 60 was the only place in the area not waterlogged and a French 3 by 2 feet mine gallery was extended. Experienced miners from Northumberland and Wales were recruited for the digging and the British attack began on 17 April 1915.

German attacks on the hill in early May included the use of gas shells and they recovered the ground at the second attempt on 5 May. It remained in their hands until 1917, when two of the mines in the Battle of Messines were detonated beneath Hill 60 and the Caterpillar.

An Ironbridge-area casualty who fought at Hill 60:
The entry is brief in the Wrekin Honour Roll and reads as follows:

> *8996 Private Cecil DAVIES, 2nd Battalion, KSLI. Eldest son of Mr E. Davies, 26 The Wharfage. Ironbridge. Killed in action at Hill 60, Ypres, 25th April 1915. Enlisted in 1908, served for 4 years in India. Took part in all the engagements in which his Battalion had been involved.*

Gallipoli, April-December 1915 – the Third Front that never was
Of all the campaigns fought in the First World War, perhaps the one that evokes the most emotive reaction is Gallipoli.

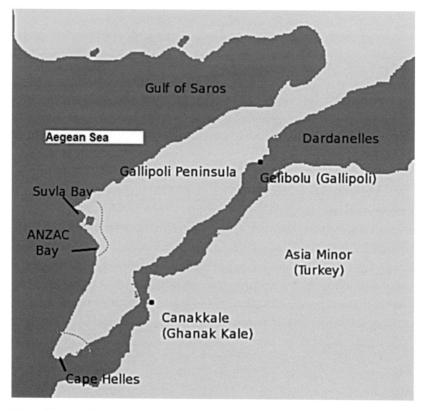

Map of Dardanelles / Gallipoli – circa 1915

As the stalemate on the Western Front dragged on through 1915, Russia had been petitioning the Allies since the previous October for help with supplies and manpower on the Eastern Front to fight the combined forces of Germany and her allies. This appeal was raised in the Commons by Winston Churchill and some of his fellow MPs who asked what the UK was doing to relieve this eastern second front with a secure supply route of men and munitions. The solution appeared to present itself in the form of a military campaign, perhaps to open up a third front, in the Turkish-held Dardanelles. This narrow strait ran past the headland and town of Gallipoli on the western peninsula. The next phase was to then press on across the sea of Marmara to capture the greater prize of Constantinople (now Istanbul) which was the gateway via the Bosphorus to the Russian ports grouped around the Black Sea beyond. It was inevitable that this region (Europe on the borders of Asia) would attract Allied attention as it was seen as a key area of contention.

First Lord of the Admiralty Churchill presented this strategy to Asquith, and the War Office, led by Kitchener, initially rejected it. He had originally envisioned the operation as a naval one but the case was made by the military commanders that it was only feasible if an infantry landing was made to secure the rugged Gallipoli peninsula. In order to muster enough infantry the British had to draw on colonial divisions from India, Australia & New Zealand Army Corps (Anzacs), which took six weeks. In the intervening period the Turkish forces, in the order of two divisions commanded by a then unknown Kemal Attaturk, had ample time to prepare. After all, this attack was not entirely unexpected by the Germans, who obviously realised its strategic importance and therefore prepared accordingly. Their German military advisor was General Otto Liman von Sanders, who kept his forces at bay until any and all British or Allied assault strategy was evident before committing them to devastating effect.

Although approved by Asquith's cabinet and Lord Kitchener the first landings at Cape Helles in the Dardanelles did not take place until 24 April. The fundamental weakness in this plan was the shortage of Allied supplies in terms of available men and materials and crucially the lack of accurate intelligence.

The major war effort was being conducted on the European mainland and this secondary campaign was viewed with disdain by the British and Allied high commands. It was regarded as a distraction from beating the Germans where it mattered most – the Western Front. During the run-up to the commencement of the operation, on March 18, as if in augury of things to come, the Allies suffered the loss of two British frigates and a French submarine to German sea-mines laid in the Dardanelle Straits.

This disastrous omen should have sounded alarm bells but was apparently overlooked in the quest for victorious results despite shortages in all manner of supplies caused by current war demands. Combined British and French forces landed on Cape Helles on the scheduled date, 24 April, enjoying initial success moving inland until superior Turkish forces pushed them back to the beach area. The terrain of flat narrow beaches overlooked by soaring promontories meant that relatively light artillery and infantry fire could keep larger forces pinned down at the waterline. While this was ongoing the Anzacs landed on the Aegean coast at a small inlet they now called Anzac Bay. The same situation unfolded causing seventy per cent casualties over their two landing beaches. Although progressing inland they could not halt the Turkish counter-attack which almost resulted in them being pushed back into the sea.

A stalemate resulted, lasting through May and June during which both sides fought to a standstill. In the torrid heat dysentery and typhoid became rife and claimed as many Allied lives as the fighting. The shortage of supplies became so desperate for the Allies that they began improvising munitions by adapting used tin cans from provisions and converting them into crude hand grenades.

The British forces commander Sir Ian Hamilton, although a capable officer, was quick to blame others for the disaster. His own plans did not bear close examination, being too complicated, relying on too many objectives being captured independently of others. Hamilton's replacement, Sir Charles Munro, assessed the situation and advised withdrawal. After much agonising through September and into October, the Cabinet and Whitehall agreed. Miraculously the Allied evacuation took place casualty-free at night through December and then into January 1916.

This was the only part of the entire operation that ran smoothly. The Turkish forces were aware of the operation but did nothing to hinder it. The eventual cost of the Gallipoli campaign was over 250,000 Allied casualties which included 27,000 French; the Anzacs suffered 35,000 casualties overall with 5,000 killed or wounded on the first day, making it the worst disaster in their history and giving rise to a continuing annual commemoration service called appropriately ANZAC day.

Ironbridge-area casualties of the Gallipoli campaign:
Coalbrookdale
Corporal Herbert J. Marshall, *New Zealand Expeditionary Force. Son of Mr Marshall, stationmaster at Coalbrookdale. Killed in action, aged 33, before 28 August 1915 at the Dardanelles. Came over with the NZ contingent, but some years previously was a pattern-maker at Coalbrookdale Works and was a member of the Ironbridge Rowing Club, having won the Kynnersley Cup for sculling. I have been unable to trace any further details.*

Madeley
L/N 19725 Lieutenant John Spencer Ruscombe Anstice. *Royal Fusiliers (City of London Regiment). Only son of Colonel Sir Arthur Anstice, formerly of Marnwood, Ironbridge. Killed in action in the Dardanelles 2 May 1915, age 21. Educated at Eton and Sandhurst, commissioned and gazetted into his regiment in September 1913. On the outbreak of war was with his regiment in India. Posted with the BEF to the Dardanelles.*

Born to such a prominent local family, his death was duly mentioned in the press. The *Journal* dated 8 May 1915 was to report the following:

Sir Arthur Anstice's Son Killed
The sad news was received at Shrewsbury yesterday that Lieut. J.S.R. Anstice Royal Fusiliers (City of London Regiment)

who was with the BEF in the Dardanelles had been killed in action. He was the only son of Colonel Sir Arthur Anstice KCB, VD, The Old Grange, Dymock, Gloucestershire, formerly of Marnwood, Ironbridge, an alderman of the Salop County Council, who commanded for many years the 1st VB, Shropshire L.I. and is chairman of the Gloucestershire Territorial Force Association. Lieut. Anstice received his commission in September 1913 and on the outbreak of the war was with his regiment in India.

Second Lieutenant Frederick Charles Youden, *15th Battalion, Australian Imperial Forces, formerly a captain in the 4th Battalion, King's Shropshire Light Infantry. Third son of Mr & Mrs John Youden, 3, Beechwood Drive, Jordanhill, Glasgow, formerly of Madeley. Killed in action at Gallipoli, 8 August 1915, aged 33. Commemorated at Lone Pine Memorial.*

Battle of Loos, 25 September to 8 October – the first great slaughter

The third battle of Artois, or Loos as it became known, was a rout for the BEF as 59,000 BEF casualties resulted out of the 285,000 total for 1915. This was the first and largest engagement of the New Army contingent (Kitchener's volunteers) and these unseasoned infantrymen were overcome by a superior force. The Germans also took the initiative and built a second line to their trenches, thereby making their storming by the BEF and Allied forces twice as difficult and problematical, resulting in increased casualties. Loos is also noted for being the first British use of chlorine gas – not wholly successful as half blew back and injured the BEF's own troops. The final tally revealed that the BEF and Allied forces casualties were twice that of the Germans.

The inevitable result, even after supplementary forces were brought in by the Allies, was another stalemated outcome. The fighting could have continued beyond the final deadline of 8 October but both sides needed to consolidate losses and objectives.

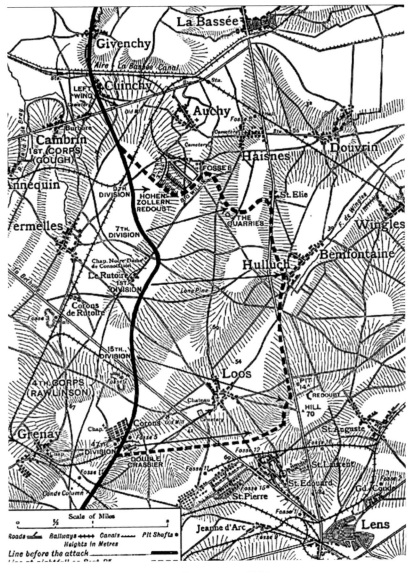

Map of Battle of Loos – Artois area, France, circa 1915

Insufficient BEF artillery shelling caused a lack of firing rate which meant the infantry could not be properly supported and positions could not be consolidated when the inevitable German counter-attacks came.

Ironbridge-area casualties of the Loos campaign
S/11748 Private John ARMSTRONG

5th Battalion, The Cameron Highlanders. Son of Mr Armstrong, 32, Wesley Road, Ironbridge. Killed in action at Loos, 25 September 1915. A member of Ironbridge Church choir, he went to live with his sister at Hawick where he was an apprentice in the hosiery mills, but joined the Camerons on the outbreak of war. He died age 21.

11593 Private Harry HANLEY, 5th Battalion KSLI, lived at Ironbridge. Died at the home of his brother-in-law Mr H. Dodd, Hodge Bower, Ironbridge, 1 December 1921, from effects of war. Wounded at the Battle of Loos, was brought back to England and spent twelve months in Brighton Hospital before being discharged from the army in 1916. He had been in poor health since. Full military funeral, buried in St. Michael's Church graveyard, Madeley. Died age 34.

Recruitment of women in UK industry

Lloyd George was appointed by Prime Minister Herbert Asquith to the brand new cabinet post of Munitions Minister in 1915. This was specially created to solve the problem of the inadequate supply of war materials and crucially munitions by reforming industrial practices and increasing output. The heavier industries of iron and steel fabrication, comprising almost exclusively male jobs, were reaching critical levels due to lack of manpower as all eligible men were volunteered to fight.

This was a key event in female emancipation as it was instrumental in breaking down industrial barriers to their employment in factories by harnessing the skills of businessmen and short-circuiting trades union disapproval. The pressing need for frontline munitions outweighed any and all prejudices in the face of mounting losses and the dire need to prosecute the war with adequate firepower.

Sir John French had commanded the BEF at the disastrous battle of Loos. His failure at this engagement, citing lack of artillery shells, plus other remarks to the press were to cost him his post.

Union opposition to the employment of women was quashed and munitions output rose dramatically so that by 1917 targeted production figures of one million heavy artillery shells per month were being regularly exceeded. This was very evidently due to the influx of female labour which was to grow dramatically so that numbers exceeded one million by 1918. For the first time in British history women were to abandon their traditional roles of home-makers and mothers.

In many cases women worked to supplement the family income due to the loss of the male pay-packet. The financial safety-net of the welfare state was many decades away and families were crucially reliant on breadwinners or family to maintain living standards in adversity. Although factory work was often heavy and exceedingly dangerous the lure of a higher wage, as well as doing their duty for their country, tipped the balance.

The Coalbrookdale company during the Great War

Much of the history of Ironbridge is founded in the Darby family who, via Abraham Darby I's pioneering smelting work using charcoal, went on through successive heirs to reach the third son to bear the forename, Abraham III, who set up the Dale company in Coalbrookdale.

This once pioneering company under the chairmanship of Alfred Darby (which was later to become Allied Ironfounders in 1929) conducted its business through the Great War making casings for aerial bombs, hand grenades, field gun carriages and cold forged brake blocks.

The company were formerly known for their cast iron fireplaces and decorative majolica-ware. Their Coalbrookdale works (nowadays partly occupied by the AGA group) was one of the first companies to employ women workers. This bold step forward in industrial relations was necessitated due to the pressing need for munitions at the front and the chronic shortage of manpower on the production line. With the introduction of conscription starting in February 1916 a drastic further reduction was apparent almost immediately. In the Coalbrookdale factory the female workforce were involved in secret

Above: *Coalbrookdale Company, now museum featuring munitionettes display, 2018*

Below: *Munitionettes at the Coalbrookdale company, with male foreman, circa 1916*

war work making shell casings to supply the BEF artillery's hungry guns as well as aerial bomber shell casings for the fledgling RFC. This qualified them to be known as 'munitionettes'.

The relaxation of working practices during wartime brought with it greater freedoms for women and also greater earning power which applied not just to manufacturing but all the service industries. This was to lead to the eventual full emancipation of women's rights, from which there was to be no going back.

Coalbrookdale company's Munitionettes
The women at the Dale End Factory worked on heavy metal castings, used in the making of parts for gun carriages and for aerial bomb casings.

The filling of these shells was undertaken at licensed explosives factories around the UK. The whole female workforce across the UK armaments industry were dubbed munitionettes but the particular women who worked to fill the shells and bombs were called 'canaries'. This was not a flattering term but due to the yellow tinge to their skin from contamination by contact with the

Munitionettes posed with bomb casings at the Coalbrookdale Company, c.1916

high explosive known as TNT. This was a poisonous chemical agent absorbed into the skin, and continued exposure was often fatal. Over 400 deaths were recorded due to overexposure to TNT throughout the Great War period, attributable to lax safety standards and the absence of protective clothing when handling explosives. By 1917 eighty per cent of shell case filling, fuses and trench supplies work was done by women. Women were also engaged in heavy engineering jobs such as building engines and operating overhead cranes and lorries. Besides being strenuous these jobs were dangerous and accidents were frequent. The other hazard was spontaneous explosion caused by the unstable nature of these explosive materials, with several serious incidents occurring across the UK. The worst was in 1917 at Silvertown in the east end of London which killed 73 people, injured many more, and destroyed or badly damaged 900 houses.

Due to this worry women started leaving the industry so the Ministry of Munitions created a Health and Welfare section to maintain production and stop the migration of skilled personnel. Laws were passed to force employers to supply safety equipment: protective clothing, seats in workrooms, washing facilities, drinking water and cloakrooms. Some employers were lax in introducing these basic measures and suffered the resultant legal consequences.

General War News: recruitment in the Ironbridge area
The following is a letter from the king to labourer William Owen, which appeared in the *Journal* of 22 May 1915. It was no doubt intended as a morale booster and encouragement to enlistment:

> *Iron-Bridge*
> *The King's Thanks:*
> *Mr. William Owen, labourer, Iron-bridge, has this week received the following letter from Buckingham Palace:-*
> *'I am commanded by the king to convey to you an expression of his Majesty's appreciation of the patriotic spirit which has prompted your six sons to give their services to the army.*

The king was much gratified to hear of the manner in which they have so readily responded to the call of their Sovereign and their country, and I am to express to you and to them his Majesty's congratulations on having contributed in so full a measure to the great cause for which all the people of the British Empire are so bravely fighting.'

The fate of all William Owen's six sons in the Great War is unclear – with the exception of one. The Wrekin Roll of Honour was to record the following:

200324 Private Robert OWEN, *7th Battalion KSLI. Son of Mr W. Owen, 18, New Bridge Road, Ironbridge. Died of wounds in France, 24 October 1918.*

CHAPTER 3

1916: Bedlam – In the thick of it

*'This cannot be considered severe in view of the numbers
engaged and the length of the front attacked.'*
(Earl Sir Douglas Haig's diary entry for 2 July 1916 on
hearing of the BEF casualties on the first day of the Somme)

Conscription introduced in the UK, 27 January to 2 March
As the battle-casualty lists mounted it was realised as early as 1915
that a steady stream of recruits was going to be needed to fill the
gaps in the British infantry lines. The appalling casualty rate up to
1916 had seen the BEF's original contingent strength of officers
and men in 1914 virtually wiped out. With little choice remaining,
Asquith's war cabinet had to bring in legislation to sustain manpower.
Consequently conscription was introduced, which required every
eligible fit man between certain ages to report for war duty.

The Military Service Act of 27 January 1916 brought conscription
into effect for the duration of the war. Along with the Defence of
the Realm Act, it was the most important piece of legislation in
placing Britain on a 'total war' footing.

Once the full recruitment campaign had started to gather steam,
another shocking statistic emerged. Over forty per cent of enlistees
were rejected for being classified as medically unfit for duty simply
because they were malnourished.

On average it took three months to train a raw recruit and even
longer to battle harden him against the horrors of the Western Front.
Although numbers swelled to nearly two million men in the time

leading up to the Somme campaign, the proportion of experienced infantrymen to raw recruits was roughly four to one. This was to weigh heavily on the effectiveness of the army that faced the *Kaiserheer* (Kaiser's Army), which was much more professional and highly trained.

Allied progress in the War: a trial of strength

1916 was to be a huge turning point for the Allies, although they did not recognise it at the time. Marshal Joseph Joffre's position as commander of a weakened French army compelled him to seek ever closer Allied cooperation with Haig and the BEF.

The French were soon to be embroiled in their own fight for survival which was to drain their manpower, weaken the Allied forces still further, and take their fighting resolve to breaking point. Concentrated around the French centrepiece military complex at Verdun it was to be struggle that would last for several months

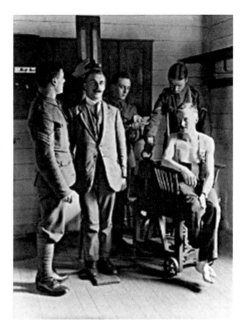

Enlistment medical fitness examination c.1916

Marshal Joseph Joffre c.1916

The year would prove to be a turning point for the Germans as well. Their High Command foolishly backed their Chief of Staff General Erich von Falkenhayn's attempt to remove the French from the war at Verdun, 'to drain their lifeblood dry', and consequently paid too high a price.

The War at Sea: Battle of Jutland, 31 May, 1916
The first and last major naval battle

At the time of the Great war, Britain operated the biggest navy in the world. The UK deemed freedom of the Channel and the North

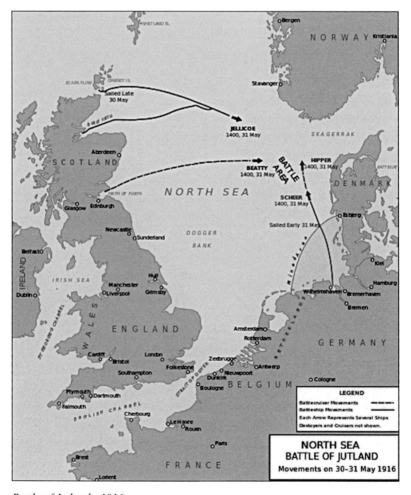

Battle of Jutland - 1916

Sea to be paramount to its naval control of the oceans and domestic sea routes thus providing a buffer zone against any threat. Its navy was a deterrent to any who wished to compromise the UK's position in the world as well as its colonial interests. Dominance of the seaways was also seen as vital in controlling any conflict worldwide. Therefore naval power dominated strategic planning, as it did in many other European nations, particularly Germany. The struggle for maritime supremacy had begun in the early years of the twentieth century with the introduction of the Dreadnought class of battleships. These were gigantic ships, commissioned by all the leading nations including America and Japan, and bristling with gun turrets that could hurl a shell the weight of a small car many miles.

Since the war's outbreak the Royal Navy had been looking for a chance to prove superiority over Germany once and for all. Admiral John Jellicoe had recently been appointed by Churchill in his capacity as First Sea Lord of the Admiralty with the note of caution that if he were not careful he could lose the war in an afternoon.

HMS Dreadnought, *circa 1906*

On the day of the Jutland sea battle the British Grand fleet's superiority seemed overwhelming. The Royal Navy deployed 151 ships of the line, compared to the German High Seas fleet which could only muster 99.

The naval commanders in this titanic power struggle were Admiral Jellicoe; his second in command, Vice Admiral Sir David Beatty; versus *Vizeadmiral* Reinhard Scheer; and his second in command *Vizeadmiral* Franz von Hipper of the *Kriegsmarine*.

Beatty began the engagement on 31 May by sailing from his base in Rosyth to chase down von Hipper's Battlecruiser force (40 ships) with his cruisers (52 ships). He did so without waiting for Jellicoe's main force to arrive from the Fleet's HQ at the Orkney Island base of Scapa Flow, two hours steaming time away. Unaware of the trap being set for him, Beatty engaged Hipper's force at 15:48 hours some 75 miles from the Danish coast. Pursuing them south-east, within an hour he had managed to lose three major ships of the line: HMS *Indefatigable* (1,017 casualties), HMS *Queen Mary* (1,266 casualties), and *Invincible* (1,026 casualties). This was over half the total of British dead at Jutland. He then found himself in the face of the rest of the High Seas Fleet as

Admiral Sir John Jellicoe

Vice-Admiral
Sir David Beatty

the German trap closed. Beatty was compelled rapidly to retreat to try to lure the Germans towards Jellicoe's main battle force sailing southwards.

Once reunited with Beatty, Jellicoe was to adopt the classic formation called 'crossing the T' thus enabling him to bring maximum firepower to bear on the advancing Germans. This manoeuvre entailed laying his warships broadside across the path of the approaching German fleet. Realising he was about to engage the entire Grand Fleet, Scheer turned his ships and fled. Due to some signalling confusion by the Royal Navy during their hasty pursuit, Scheer and his remaining fleet managed to slip away under cover of darkness.

It was immediately claimed as a victory by both sides. The British came off far worse with a total of 14 ships lost and 6,094 dead as opposed to Germany's losses of 10 ships for 2,551 dead. But when the Kaiser learned of these losses he forbade the High

Seas Fleet to ever sail again. This startling decision resulted in a strategic victory for the Royal Navy.

One outcome for the British navy was the banning of the practice of leaving a ship's magazine bay fire safety doors open to increase the rapidity of shell delivery to the gun turrets above in order to match the rate of fire, as it left ships' magazines vulnerable to stray sparks and hot shrapnel from exploding incoming shells.

Ironbridge-area casualties at the Battle of Jutland

The entry in the Wrekin District Roll of Honour reads:

> *K/ 14764 Stoker First Class, Thomas W. NICKLESS*, *Royal Navy.*
> *Son of Mr. Samuel Nickless, 30, Lincoln Hill, Ironbridge. He was killed in action on board HMS Acasta at the Battle of Jutland, 31st May 1916.*

Thomas had served four years in the navy and although his ship was not sunk he was one of six killed on board. He previously worked for the Coalbrookdale Company.

Here is the story of Thomas Nickless's ship:

HMS *Acasta* at Jutland

Thomas Nickless's ship HMS *Acasta* was the name ship of the Acasta class destroyer of the Royal Navy. She was built between 1911 and 1913, and was initially designated a K-class boat destroyer having at various times the pennant numbers G40, H59 (1914) or H00 (1918). The ship was originally intended to be named HMS *King*, was laid down at John Brown's shipyard at Clydebank on 1 December 1911, launched on 10 September 1912, and completed the following month. Powered by two Brown-Curtis steam turbines she had a maximum speed of 32 knots and had a complement of 75-77 men. After completion she joined the 4th Destroyer Flotilla. *Acasta* served with the Grand Fleet from the outbreak of the First World War. On 16 December 1914 she was in the 4th Destroyer Flotilla attached to a battle group sent to challenge several German ships which bombarded the North Yorkshire

HMS Acasta *(destroyer of the* Acasta *class) circa 1915*

coast, causing damage to Whitby, Scarborough and Hartlepool, which collectively suffered 119 civilian deaths. During the Battle of Jutland the 4th Flotilla was attached to Admiral David Beatty's Battlecruiser Fleet based at Rosyth and assigned to cover the Third Battle Cruiser Squadron screening the cruiser HMS *Chester*. HMS *Acasta* was under the command of Lieutenant Commander J.O. Barron as she joined the squadron that left Pentland Firth on the evening of 30 May 1916, finally engaging the enemy at 5.40pm on 31 May. During the battle, destroyer HMS *Shark* was crippled by gunfire and was offered assistance by the already damaged *Acasta* but declined.

During the same action, against a superior enemy force, *Acasta* was hit by two 5.9-inch shells from SMS *Derfflinger* which left her with six crewmen dead including Tom Nickless and one wounded, and unable to stop or steer. A signal from HMS *Benbow* at 6.40pm reported that *Acasta* was in danger of sinking.

Admiral Beatty's report on the battle mentions an unknown, disabled destroyer which, from the time (about 7pm) may refer to *Acasta*. At 6.47pm Jellicoe's HMS *Iron Duke*, the Grand Fleet's flagship, passed the disabled destroyer whose crew lined the sides to cheer the battleship as she passed. *Acasta* was able to effect some emergency repairs during the next six hours, but broke down again and was eventually taken in tow by HMS *Nonsuch* and reached Aberdeen two days after the battle, so badly damaged she practically had to be rebuilt.

She claimed a torpedo hit on SMS *Lutzow* but this was not officially confirmed.

The German Admiralty's report of the battle on 1 June included the claim that *Acasta* had been destroyed. Despite her brave service *Acasta*'s ultimate fate was to be broken up for scrap in 1921.

HMS *Acasta* fatalities suffered at the Battle of Jutland:
- Engineer: Lieutenant James Forrest
- Chief Petty Officer: Stoker Richard Massey
- Chief Stoker: G. Howe
- Engine Room Artificer: James Bailey
- Stoker 1: Thomas William Nickless, of Ironbridge
- Signalman: Thomas Jordan

Another Ironbridge casualty of the Battle of Jutland was:

Alfred WHITEHEAD, *Royal Navy. Son of Joseph Whitehead, Head Baker at Ironbridge Co-op Wholesale Society. Lost at sea on HMS Queen Mary at the Battle of Jutland, 31st May 1916. Joined the Navy prior to the outbreak of war and after leaving the training ship HMS Impregnable was transferred to the Queen Mary. Died at age 17.*

Death of Kitchener

Journal edition of 16 June 1916 printed the syndicated news report complete with verse, that was to shock the nation and the people of the Ironbridge area:

Lord Herbert Horatio Kitchener,
circa 1915

The Empire's Great Loss
Lord Kitchener Drowned
Leaving in battle no blot on his name
Looks proudly to heaven from the death-bed of fame
The whole Empire was shocked this week with the news that Field-Marshal Lord Kitchener Secretary of State for War and one of the foremost military organisers in the world had lost his life by drowning. On the invitation of the Czar, Lord Kitchener had undertaken a visit to Russia to discuss important military and financial questions when the vessel on which he was travelling, the armoured cruiser HMS Hampshire, was sunk west of the Orkneys by a mine or torpedo. Four boats were seen to leave the sinking ship, but heavy seas were running and only a raft containing one warrant officer and 11 men of the crew has come ashore.

Accompanying Lord Kitchener were Sir H.F. Donaldson of the Ministry of Munitions, Brig. Gen. W. Ellershaw; Mr H. J. O'Beirne, of the Foreign office; & Lt. Col. D. A. Fitzgerald C.M.G. (personal military secretary to Lord

Kitchener) whose body has been washed up. Messages from all quarters testify to the deep sense of loss sustained.

HMS Hampshire was an armoured cruiser of the County Class of 10,850 tons built at Elswick in 1905. The total estimated cost of the ship including guns was £856,527. Her principal armament was four 7.5-inch guns, six 6-inch guns and twenty 3-pounders. She carried a complement of 655 men.

By the death of Earl Kitchener the army loses a commander whose name and fame were only less potent than those of the late Lord Roberts, the ministry a great organiser and a resolute administrator, and the empire one of its leading citizens. He has died in harness - not on the field of battle as he would probably have wished, yet surrounded by his staff and at the hands of his country's enemies.

The nation was devastated at such a loss, but Whitehall drew a collective sigh of relief. Prime Minister Asquith's wife was heard to privately remark that 'as a war-leader he made a great recruiting poster.

Lloyd George meets Earl Haig in France

The vital cabinet post of Minister for War needed to be filled and filled quickly, by just as nationally charismatic a leader as Kitchener, to sustain the nation's resolve.

David Lloyd George seemed the only candidate with enough charisma to galvanise the nation and the war effort. He was therefore appointed by Asquith to the post on 6 June 1916. He immediately set about visiting Haig at his HQ at Montreuil-sur-Mer. France.

Upon meeting face to face, a mutual dislike transpired that was to shape their relationship for the rest of the war. Lloyd George took his man to be impetuous, foolhardy and prone to wilfully ignoring governmental directives. Haig adopted the prevalent military view of disregarding the advice of Whitehall and in particular Lloyd George's; he considered it meddlesome interference in a war that was too important to be left to politicians. On paper at least, Lloyd George was proved right, given what was to come when the next chapter in the war unfolded, on the Somme river in France.

The Western Front: Battle of the Somme, 1 July to 18 November

Destined to be forever known in the annals of history as a byword for slaughter, the term 'the battle of the Somme' is a historical misnomer. It was not a single battle or engagement but a long campaign consisting of a series of attritional battles welded together in the overarching Allied planning strategy.

Although originally intended by the Allies to be completed within six weeks, this notorious campaign was to last from 1 July to 18 November of 1916. This was due to a catastrophic underestimation of the strength and resilience of the opposing German forces. The affected area of Picardy in northern France, which comprised several villages plus an ancient chateau, known collectively as the Thiepval estates, was totally obliterated over the course of the campaign, which was destined to last four and a half months. The bones of these nine villages were to be further raked over in successive campaigns throughout the war.

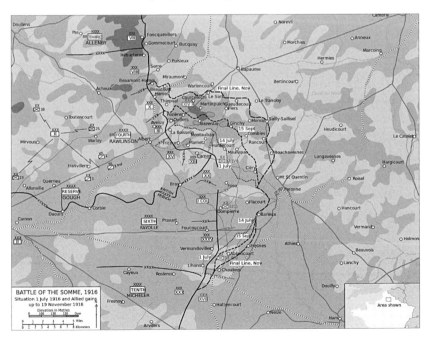

Main battlefield area of the Somme: c.1916

The overall Somme campaign was intricately planned and detailed by Haig's second in command General Herbert Rawlinson. This brilliant yet egocentric officer, like his superior, did not take well to criticism. Haig was focused on results at any cost and the pressing need as he saw it to beat back the Germans to the Belgian coast. Once there he planned to capture the Belgian ports from which the Germans were launching their U-boat campaigns to harass Allied shipping. Success on the Somme would hinder their progress and undermine their psychological advantage, or so Haig reasoned.

The Allied French commander General Joffre also badly needed this success to break the stalemate and raise the morale of his officers and men. He had originally selected the area of the Somme as a relatively quiet area to attack. However the area was very heavily fortified and its German tenants, 3rd Bavarian, had occupied their trenches since the end of the second battle of Ypres in March 1915 – plenty of time for the Bosch engineers to fully plumb in their trenches making them virtually impregnable. Most had their own electricity supply and were lined with bomb-proof bricks and concrete to a depth of ten metres. A second line of trenches was later added with buildings and fortifications placed every twenty metres made into blockhouses doubling as command centres, guard posts and machine gun emplacements.

Originally the campaign had been planned as a joint venture with the French who were to take the lead. However as the crisis deepened at Verdun the French were obliged to commit more and more men and equipment to the fight leaving the British with an ever bigger and more exposed role at the Somme. This forced Haig to commit the raw untried recruits of the BEF's volunteer and conscripted army which comprised 75 per cent of the available strength.

The Somme campaign's main weakness was that there were too many objectives to be captured, even on the first day, with not enough thought given to how to consolidate territorial gains and frustrate the inevitable German counter-response. As the smoke cleared from the BEF Royal Artillery's seven-day barrage, ending on 30 June, the infantry line, stretching twenty-four miles, prepared themselves for a mass attack along the north of the river while the

French intended a similar manoeuvre to the south. Whistles blew at 7:30am on Saturday, 1 July, and the first infantry wave, led by their junior officers (usually of second lieutenant rank), 'went over the top', in a mostly vain attempt to cross no man's land.

Every infantryman carried an assault pack containing on average 60 lbs of equipment comprising trenching tools, gas capes, ammunition including two Mills bombs (hand-grenades), and field rations, along with a 303 Lee Enfield single bolt-action rifle equipped with twenty-four rounds and an eighteen-inch fitted steel bayonet. The pack weight and confusion of noise and smoke led to a disorientated scramble for the infantryman across a landscape pockmarked with shell craters. Once he had entered no-man's land there were other perilous hazards such as barbed-wire and explosive booby-traps designed to catch out the unwary attacker. They were ordered not to break ranks but to walk slowly towards the enemy trenches and definitely not to charge at breakneck speed – so as to conserve energy. Unfortunately this instruction allowed the German machine guns to wreak a remorseless destruction upon them.

Underneath the battleground further weaponry development produced yet more subtle and diverse systems of warfare such as the wired landmine. Just before the initial BEF assault, at 07:20 hours, the attack began with the detonation of a gigantic mine placed under the German lines. This was laid by the Royal Engineers tunnelling unit under Hawthorn Ridge Redoubt, near Beaumont-Hamel, at the beginning of what the Allies called the the Battle of Albert. The mine was a 6,600 lb monster and was recorded as the biggest blast in human history, and rumoured to have been heard as far away as London. Some of the nineteen biggest mines ever used were exploded on the first day of the Somme by BEF sapper units comprising coal miners burrowing under the German lines.

The Hawthorn Ridge Redoubt mine explosion was filmed from a BEF position by cinematographer Geoffrey Malins who set his camera up half a mile away. A single frame from his film became one of the iconic photographs depicting the first day of the battle.

Trench-mine blast, Hawthorn Ridge Redoubt, 1 July 1916, Somme

The Germans were able to mostly repel the BEF advance despite suffering heavy casualties. The official BEF casualty figure, collated by the Adjutant General's office on 2 July, amounted to 19,241 dead in the field with 47,600 wounded, missing or captured. It is still regarded as the worst day in the British army's history from the standpoint of number of casualties to ground captured.

The offensive was destined to grind on through a series of attritional battles until 18 November, culminating in the battle of Beaumont-Hamel, which was originally a day-one objective. Winter finally called a halt to the hostilities. Subsequent German counter-offensives retook all the ground captured, a meagre seven miles, which in turn was retaken by the Allies in 1918. In terms of fighting men the final overall figures were staggering. The Allies suffered 427,000 declared casualties overall, the Germans upwards of 630,000.

The largest war graves cemetery at Thiepval was to be adorned with the famous memorial to the missing designed by Sir Edwin Lutyens which lists over 72,000 names of the BEF designated as missing with no known grave.

Ironbridge area: casualties of the Somme campaign

The Wrekin Honour Roll testifies to the extent of local casualties as follows:

3548 Private Frank Sorton Downing, 2/6th Battalion, Royal Warwickshire Regiment. Husband of Mrs. A. Downing Wellington Road, Coalbrookdale. Eldest son of John Downing, 23, Dale End, Coalbrookdale. Died of wounds in France, 1st July 1916. Age 26, he enlisted in November 1914, prior to which he was a cabinet-maker employed at Birmingham. Former bell-ringer at Coalbrookdale Parish Church.

23735 Private William Henry Edwards, 7th Battalion KSLI. Born at Madeley, lived at Ironbridge. Killed in action at the Battle of Ancre, Somme campaign 13th November 1916.

27760 Private William Edward Hall, Border Regiment, son of George Hall, Sycamore House, Ironbridge, later of 15, Church Hill, Ironbridge. Killed in action on the Somme, 18th November 1916. Formerly a moulder at Coalbrookdale Works. He joined the colours on 8th March 1915 and had only been in France for 6 weeks. Considered one of the best bowlers in the Ironbridge District League. Age 26. Formerly 4996 Herefordshire Regiment.

53133 Private John Jones, 19th Battalion, King's Liverpool Regiment. Born & lived at Jackfield. Killed in action in Flanders 12th October 1916 (Somme Campaign).

6969 Private Benjamin Owen, 11th Battalion, The Sherwood Foresters (Nottingham & Derbyshire Regiment). Born at

Dawley, lived in Ironbridge. Killed in action Flanders, 30th July 1916 (Somme Campaign).

*135624 **Private Bertie Reginald Perry**, 1st Battalion, Canadian Mounted Rifles. Eldest son of Mr Samuel Perry, Woodside, Coalbrookdale. Killed in action France 15th September 1916 (Somme Campaign).*

*31122 **Lance Corporal George Reynolds**, 6th Battalion, South Staffordshire Regiment. Husband of Mrs. A. Reynolds, 252 Werps Road, Jackfield. Killed in action at Regina Trench, Thiepval, France, 21st October 1916. Son of Arthur.*

*12207 **Private Thomas Rogers**, 6th Battalion, KSLI, Son of Mrs Rogers of Ironbridge. Killed in action on the Somme, 30th June 1916.*

*14394 **Sergeant Richard Everard Buckworth-Herne-Soame**, The Depot KSLI. Elder son of Sir Charles Buckworth-Herne-Soame, 5 Cherry Tree Hill, Coalbrookdale. Died of wounds at Kempston Hospital, Eastbourne, 30th July 1916. Seriously wounded in action (on the Somme), he was brought back to hospital in Eastbourne but succumbed to his wounds. After a military funeral was interred at Ocklynge Cemetery.*

*17950 **Private William Ambrose Wright**, 5th Battalion KSLI. Husband to Mrs Margaret Wright, 6, Ladywood, Ironbridge, formerly of Madeley. Killed in action at Delville Wood, on the Somme, 23rd August 1916. Before enlisting he worked as a tile-presser at Messrs. Prestage's works, Jackfield. Aged 40, he left a widow and 7 children.*

Total Warfare: Lloyd George's Creed

Although appalled at the attritional tactics that Haig employed against the Germans and the lack of progress, Lloyd George was

David Lloyd George PM,
circa 1916

the first politician to preach the mantra of total war in the conflict. He said in an interview with journalist Roy Clarke in September 1916 that the war must be fought to the finish, delivering a knockout blow to the Germans. It was a theme he would return to many times over the course of the war. This became the Lloyd George's 'Total War' creed.

This aspirational wartime ideal ensured that Britain survived the war's tragedies with a resilient spirit, a determination to win and a modern industrial strategy that was to prove so crucial in the later conflict of the Second World War.

Tribunal hearings in the Ironbridge area, 1916-18

After the introduction of conscription from March 1916 most UK newspapers carried reports of exemption tribunals. These were pseudo-military formal local hearings held across the UK and designed to virtually intimidate men into enlisting. Though tacked onto the Petty Session hearings, their legal authority was highly dubious.

There were defined categories of enlistees such as minimum and maximum age limits of 19 to 45, others being considered exempt. However, occupations were constantly under review to adjudge whether they were war service exempt or not. Presiding adjudicators worked from paperwork supplied by the army listing those local men who had failed to answer their formal letters of conscription, as well as those petitioning anew for exemption on the grounds of vital war work under the newly-coined phrase 'reserved occupation'.

The following extracts are drawn from editions of the *Journal* detailing the supposed growing problem locally (including some big names such as Maw & Co and Coalport China Co).

The *Journal* edition dated 3 June 1916 reported the following:

IRON-BRIDGE
Borough Tribunal – Monday *– Messrs Dyas, Maw, Hobson, Nicklin, Clarke-Bruff (military representative), Ainsworth (farmers representative) Potts (Town Clerk) presiding. – A china company made application for a packer and a London manager. Mr Maw was of the opinion that a packer was a reserved occupation – Mr Bott who represented the company remarked that this was the reason of their application. After some discussion the packer was exempted for six months ...*

The *Journal* edition dated 10 June reported:

IRON-BRIDGE
Borough Tribunal: *Mr Dyas presiding:-*
A Wenlock master plumber at the Lady Forester Hospital pleaded reserved occupation and was granted six months exemption. ...

A Coalport blacksmith reported that he was the only blacksmith left between Sutton and Ironbridge – he was granted six months (conditional). ...

A Jackfield manufacturer appealed for a tile sorter. The Applicant stated that he had 44 men before the war and now there were only four – Four Months was allowed. ...

A Madeley licensed victualler made application for exemption. Having stated his case, four months exemption was granted. ...

Six months conditional exemption was granted a Jackfield manager, who it was stated had ten children. ...

A china company (Coalport China) made application on behalf of eight of their employees. It was stated that the company had 52 potters before the war and that there were only 25 left and if any more were taken the works would have to be stopped. Again only four printers were left out of eleven and four polishers out of nine. A Mr. Bott (representative for the company) told the Tribunal that 80 per cent of their business was export. He made a strong appeal for exemption, for all the men referred to. He said their business was like a chain and no links could be spared. Four months exemption was granted but the printer was entirely exempted. ...

A Madeley fishmonger asked for total exemption. He said that he had nine children – Granted.

CHAPTER 4

1917: From the Gorge into the Abyss

A Great War of attrition

1917 was proving to be a year of great vicissitudes for the Allies as no real progress was being made in the one theatre of war that mattered to politicians – the Western Front. Marshal Joffre badly needed to galvanise his forces to action as there was mutiny stirring in the ranks. The French were beset by malaise, fuelled by every kind of shortage and indifferent to bad leadership. Although remotivated by the victory at Verdun, the war so far had caused over 600,000 French casualties and the fighting had now drifted back to trench-bound stalemate.

The French army had frankly had enough; it had sacrificed its best blood many times over and lost the will to fight. On the Eastern Front the Russians were facing a backlash from their own desperate fighting men. Riots at home led to the outbreak of revolution resulting in the Tsar's forced abdication in April. In October the world's first Communist government took office and effectively ended any further participation in the war. The Tsar and his family were imprisoned and later executed, shot on Lenin's orders thus wiping out the Romanoff line forever without any possibility of a return to power. On learning of the assassination of his cousin Tsar Nicholas and his immediate family, King George V endured deep personal regret at his refusal to offer sanctuary to them when it was requested after abdicating in 1917.

Scene from Passchendaele battleground, circa 1917

The Battle of Passchendaele, (31 July to 19 November 1917)
The needless rush to victory

Haig's dogged persistence about faltering German resistance, based on his chief of intelligence Major John Charteris's dubious information, won the day among the Allied chiefs when in April he planned another attack through Picardy to break the deadlock on the Western Front.

Once triumphant, his further intention was to secure the north-western area of the front before moving on to the Belgian channel ports to disable the German submarine bases to thus alleviate the attacks on Allied merchant shipping. His campaign was codenamed the Third Battle of Ypres but was to be dubbed the Passchendaele offensive as the fighting centred around the village of Passchendaele and the Messines ridge which lay at the heart of the area. The campaign was destined to become another byword for slaughter. Even French General Ferdinand Foch and Lloyd George were against this dubious offensive from the start. Their deductions were based on some very pertinent facts. They reasoned that the expense of men and equipment to secure the ground was outweighed by its lack of possible material gain. They also pointed out that the American forces were coming on stream and therefore the Allies should wait till their total strength could be augmented to fully tackle the Germans. Then by sheer weight of numbers, the Allies would defeat them that much more quickly and comprehensively. Because of this lingering uncertainty Haig did not receive Cabinet approval until 25 July. His resolve to sweep the faltering German resistance, as he saw it, before him and reach the Belgian ports was not to be undermined.

Passchendaele duly entered the history books as the needless slaughter it became. The fighting commenced 31 July through to November and resulted in 245,000 Allied casualties which included those listed below from the Ironbridge area. As the fighting wore on, the constant back and forth of artillery bombardments destroyed the once lush forestlands across all the battlefields of the Messines salient reducing them to the semblance of a lunar landscape.

When the weather turned, the autumn rains left the ground in a further deteriorated state turning it into a mud-filled morass which was lethally hazardous to all of the troops. It was only when the Canadians finally took Vimy Ridge in Passchendaele on 10 November that the campaign effectively ended. The Germans were left with over 400,000 casualties.

It was to be the Battle of Caporetto on the Isonzo river which forced Haig to cease the Passchendaele operation, to keep Italy in the war by sending Allied forces to support their tattered army. Thus closed the military book on this disastrous campaign once and for all, leaving it second only to the Somme campaign of the previous year as the most expensive engagement in terms of casualties sustained for the least ground achieved in any battle in the annals of warfare.

Ironbridge-area casualties of Passchendaele:-
26094 Private William Baugh, 6th Battalion KSLI. Son of Mr and Mrs W. Baugh, The Lodge, Ironbridge. Died from wounds 18 August 1917 received at Ypres (Passchendaele). Shot by sniper as member of Lewis Gun team. Age 19, worked at the Severn Foundry, Coalbrookdale. Buried at Dozinghem Military Cemetery Westvleteren, Belgium.

763146 Private John Henry Benbow, 28th Battalion County of London Artists Rifles
Born and lived at Coalport. Killed in action in Flanders 30 October 1917 (Passchendaele)

30399 Private Reginald Burton, 1st Battalion, King's Own Royal Lancaster Regiment. Son of Mr E. Burton, Station Hotel, Ironbridge. Brother to Harry. Killed in action in Flanders,12 October 1917. Commemorated on Tyne Cot Memorial, Passchendaele, Belgium. Age 35.

25510 Private William Edward Cornes, 5th Battalion KSLI. Son of Mr W.E. Cornes, The Lloyds, Ironbridge. Died of wounds in France, 11 September 1917, age 19. Was formerly employed at the Coalbrookdale works and joined KSLI in November 1916.

Home Front: The battle for hearts and minds

The term 'Home Front', first coined in the Great War, was considered uniquely British.

No other participating country quite described their own civil defence measures in such terms. The expression was assumed as part of the 1915 Prime Minister Lloyd George's campaign to re-educate the people about the country's war status.

He was forever trying to change the civil mindset to one of accepting that the country needed to be set on a 'total war' footing and part of this battle would be won on home soil.

'The war is divided,' he told them, 'into two fronts. The combatant front where the war is waged against the enemy directly on the ground and the "Home" front where war is waged firstly against waste in the home particularly with food, then more importantly against drunken idleness.'

The licensing laws prior to 1915 were generous – opening time 5am through all the day until closing time at 2am (twenty-one hours of opening a day). These were changed to 6pm to 10.30pm Monday to Friday with 2pm to 10pm on weekends, and it was rigorously enforced. It was considered good for industry as drink-related absenteeism was high and workers often turned up for work in an inebriated state. They posed a risk to themselves and others when using heavy machinery and when handling explosives.

With the Defence of the Realm Act, the British people found themselves living under some draconian laws. DORA was a unique piece of legislation which controlled many aspects of a UK citizen's life, even idle gossip.

Keeping up morale

It was seen by civil and military powers as a critical morale booster, in the face of mounting losses at the battlefront, for the UK populace to witness captured enemy weaponry paraded through the streets. Here was living proof that despite all, the 'boys at the front' were doing their job. The *Journal* of 16 June 1916 describes a carnival atmosphere in the town:

> ### Iron-Bridge
> **The German Gun** – *On Saturday all the town and district turned out and witnessed the parade of the German gun captured at the battle of Loos in which the Shropshires took a brilliant part. A procession formed in the Market Square capably marshalled by Sgt. Gauton (Civic Guard Corps) in the following order: Coalbrookdale Brass band, Ironbridge & Madeley Volunteer Training Corps, Iron-Bridge, Broseley & Jackfield Fire Brigades; Ironbridge Scouts... The Gun was pulled with six horses and six men from the Leighton Remount depot... During the route the ambulance nurses and Supt. Lady Andrews, received donations for the wounded soldiers fund... The parade halted at the funfair where the takings from six rides was added to the collection... The procession reforming returned to the Square & it was here that Councillor Maddox (on behalf of Alderman Dyas) thanked all who had taken part in the procession.*

Sporting heroes at war: Ironbridge Football Club

In the battle for hearts and minds, the war was subtly likened to sport by using the sporting stars of the day who had joined

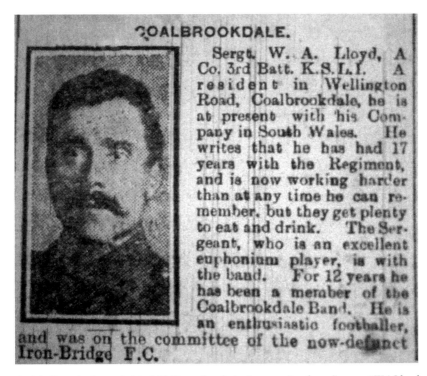

COALBROOKDALE.

Sergt. W. A. Lloyd, A Co. 3rd Batt. K.S.L.I. A resident in Wellington Road, Coalbrookdale, he is at present with his Company in South Wales. He writes that he has had 17 years with the Regiment, and is now working harder than at any time he can remember, but they get plenty to eat and drink. The Sergeant, who is an excellent euphonium player, is with the band. For 12 years he has been a member of the Coalbrookdale Band. He is an enthusiastic footballer, and was on the committee of the now-defunct Iron-Bridge F.C.

Article from the Journal *dated 21 November featuring sporting hero Sergeant W.A Lloyd*

the ranks. In Ironbridge the local football club, although a founder member of the Shropshire League (1890-91), was disbanded shortly before the war.

The following are extracts from reports in the *Journal* which track the war history of some of the players.

The *Journal* of 21 November 1914 reports on a local ex-player:

Coalbrookdale
Sergt. W.A. Lloyd, A Company, 3rd Batt. K.S.L.I. A resident in Wellington Road Coalbrookdale, he is at present with his Company in South Wales. He writes that he has had 17 years with the Regiment, and is now working harder than at any other time he can remember, but they get plenty to eat and drink. The Sergeant who is an excellent Euphonium player, is with the band. For 12 years he has been a member of the

Coalbrookdale Band. He is an enthusiastic footballer and was on the committee of the now-defunct Iron-Bridge FC.

Another report in the *Journal* dated 13 July 1918 traces three more ex-players:

Coalbrookdale
War News *– Private Sanders, late Captain of Iron-Bridge FC, is an inmate of Berrington Hospital. It appears that his football days are over, which all footballers will regret. Sanders was an expert and was always a gentleman on and off the field.*

Sergeant. A. Roden R.F.A. [Royal Field Artillery], out of three years service has seen two and a half years fighting in France & the other day had quite an experience. The horse he was riding was blown up and the poor animal fell on Arthur breaking one of his ankles. After a few weeks in Broseley Hospital he is now at Llandudno Convalescent Home and is making satisfactory progress. Sergt. Roden was also a member of the defunct Iron-Bridge FC.

Private P. Wale (Benthall Edge) who was wounded in the knee and ankle is lying in a London Hospital going on well. He too was a footballer. He has another brother serving in the forces.

Home Front: The hidden truth in plain sight
With the priority taken by war munitions, domestic food production fell dramatically.

To combat this, various local authorities opened up public ground for allotments where food cultivation was put under the control of the ordinary citizen. Long-term sustainability of supply depended on mass cultivation as farmers bemoaned the manpower shortages imposed by conscription.

The Women's Land Army was formed in 1917 by Meriel Talbot who, as the first woman inspector appointed for the Ministry of Agriculture, welded this workforce into an indispensable tool in the vital job of feeding the nation.

Wartime rationing in UK – women queuing for shop basics, circa 1917

The 'Land Girls' as they were known were given six weeks training on specially selected farms learning the basics of working agriculture and managing livestock. Some did specialised work as tractor operators, carters, thatchers, shepherds or market gardeners. The tenure of service was six months, being paid 18 shillings (90 pence) per week rising to £1 after they had passed their proficiency tests Their contribution was to last well into 1919 as the shortages prevailed and out of the 26,000 women who had worked on the land throughout the war over 23,000 saw service in the Land Army.

Rationing introduced into the UK

Rationing in one form or another came in early, and was worsened by panic buying, which was dealt with, but the situation steadily deteriorated. The U-boat campaign in the Atlantic was effective in reducing imports as Allied merchant shipping was to lose over 8 million tonnes across the duration of the war. By the end of 1916 the supply of meat and major foodstuffs was becoming a problem. This caused the government to respond by creating the Ministry of Food whose first task was to ban the export of food. Rationing of provisions was introduced in 1917, commencing with sugar, in London and the home counties and then to the rest of the country. This was followed by the issue of rationing cards for meat and fats.

Ironbridge Civil Defence Corps

In Ironbridge it was recognised soon after the UK's declaration of war that a civilian defence corps made up of local ex-soldiers and older or militarily exempt men was needed to protect domestic interests in case of invasion and keep up morale at home for the duration.

The *Journal* of 22 August 1914 reported the Ironbridge CDC formation:

> ### Iron-Bridge
> *The Mayor (Dr. G.D. Collins) presided at a public meeting last week at the Armoury, when it was decided to form a Civic Guard[5] Corps and Mr A.O. Callear was appointed secretary and Sergeant Gauton drill instructor.*

War News: Letter from an Ironbridge serviceman

The *Journal* of 9 January 1915 reads:

> ### From the Front
> *Private W. Owen,[6] of the D Company KSLI, who is with the British Expeditionary Force in France, has written to Miss F. Lloyd, President of the Ironbridge Women's Liberal Association, thanking the members for the parcel received. They could not imagine how proud he felt to be able to fight for them all, and the gifts he received from his own townspeople made him all the more fit for the campaign.*

---

5 Local titles were optional as no formal organisational guidance was issued by the government or civil authorities at this stage of the war

6 We can only speculate that this could be one of the six sons of Mr W. Owen, labourer, of Ironbridge who received a letter of thanks from the king because all his sons had enlisted together.

CHAPTER 5

1918: The Industry of Wholesale Slaughter

'We must fight with our backs to the wall.'
(Extract from Field Marshal Haig's telegram to all troops,
11 April 1918)

War machines

Historians might argue that the war's great inventions were not the game changers that led to the defeat of one of the greatest land armies in Europe, but the sheer weight of forces ranged against Germany and her allies. The Germans were more advanced and their arsenal better equipped.

British armaments were of consistent good quality with firearms such as the Lee Enfield .303 bolt-action ten-round magazine-fed rifle, the Webley Mk VI .455 calibre six-shot revolver (officer issue only), and the Vickers .303 water-cooled machine gun which comprised the BEF standard infantry issue. Although they were still in use by British armed forces up to the 1960s, all were outdated having been originally produced in the late 1800s.

The role of the machine gun

Next to shrapnel from fragmentation artillery shells, the heavy machine gun was the most devastating weapon of the war. Its mass deployment by the Germans cost hundreds of thousands of

Machine gun – BEF issue, circa 1915

Allied infantry men's lives, particularly in engagements such as the Somme and Passchendaele. At the time of the Great War the machine gun was not a new invention. The Germans deployed over 10,000 in 1914. But the BEF carried less than 200 because they were regarded by the military as insignificant to the outcome of full frontal attack, relying instead on infantry supported by cavalry to barge their way through enemy lines.

The war in the air

With the rapid development of powered flight, from its crude beginnings in 1903 with the Wright Brothers in the USA, European nations, particularly Germany, quickly recognised the potential of these 'flying machines' as weapons of war. In 1909, after the successful flight across the English Channel, a feat which attracted world attention, the Frenchman Louis Bleriot began designing and making his own aircraft and was subsequently contracted by the British to make war planes.

BE 2c RFC (RAF) fixed wing biplane, circa 1916

UK armed forces had no official organised separate air force even at the outbreak of the war. Generals consigned this new-fangled invention to the Balloon Corps division of the army. By 1918 there were 188 squadrons, and the official title Royal Air Force was instituted on 1 April of that year.

Many combat 'aces' were so dubbed for the number of 'kills' they had made in the air. Up to 1915 the only bombing of the enemy from the air was done by simply dropping hand-primed devices such as hand grenades and single bombs over the side of a two-seater light aircraft at the lowest height possible. Restrictions on payload meant the fighter was limited, but heavier capacity aircraft with the specific task of carpet-bombing enemy positions were not developed till later in the war and remained undesignated within the service until the Second World War.

Battle of Cambrai, 20 November to 7 December 1917 – first massed Allied tank attack

With its introduction at the Somme campaign the tank had announced its arrival into the armoury of war weapons. On 28 July 1917, the Heavy Branch was separated from the rest of the Machine Gun Corps by royal warrant and given official status as the Tank Corps. Cambrai was the first mass tank attack involving

Tank Corps: Mark IV type tank (male), circa 1917

nine battalions with over 430 Allied units committed. The first commander of the Tank Corps was Lieutenant General Sir Hugh Jamieson Elles. After their poor showing in the Passchendaele offensive, due to the sodden mud-covered terrain, Commander Elles suggested to Haig that greater success would be achieved on the drier, flatter, more open country around Cambrai. He successfully led 350 Mk IVs into battle, riding his own tank, called *Hilda* after a favourite aunt, adorned with the corps' pennant flag that he designed, of brown, red and green silk. Although the battle demonstrated the effectiveness of the tank in overcoming trench defences such as barbed wire, previously thought impregnable by the Germans, the overall result of the campaign was a stalemate.

The more mobile campaigns fought in the latter stages of the war would be characterised by the classic battle formation of sending tanks in first, with infantry in the rear, covered for protection from small arms fire, with the objective of mopping up enemy resistance and more importantly consolidation of ground gained. The introduction of the Tank Corps undoubtedly underscored the spectacular Allied successes of 1918 when its full complement had risen to 26 battalions.

An Ironbridge-area casualty of Cambrai
200993 Sergeant Jack GOODWIN, 5th Battalion Tank Corps. Lived at Coalbrookdale. Killed in action at Flanders 16 April 1918. Formerly 15580 in the KSLI and in the Machine Gun Corps. No known grave, commemorated on Ploegsteert Memorial.

The Allied blip on the road to victory, February to April 1918

If the overall outlook, on the western front in particular, looked gloomy at the beginning of 1917, with continued stalemate, then the position at the beginning of 1918, with shortages of every description, plaguing mainly the French but also the BEF, looked even bleaker. With the virtual collapse of the eastern front, and Germany seemingly poised to exploit the situation on the western front, it was beginning to look conceivable that Germany could win the war.

These apparent weaknesses in the Allied campaign were to be seized upon by German second in command General Erich Ludendorff who was mostly gambling on the schisms developing within the Allied ranks to pursue his own plan to subdue the Allies and secure an honourable peace.

The main protagonists, Britain and France, were running out of steam. They rested weary and wounded forces and busied themselves with consolidating positions. The French army faced open mutiny, brought on by recent losses, vital shortages and bad leadership among the officers in the field. This position was firmly resolved when newly-promoted Field Marshal Ferdinand Foch appointed Marshal Philippe Pétain to manage the discipline and morale of exhausted troops. The French had lost over 600,000 men by this point in the war, mostly at Verdun in 1916. For his part Earl Haig was also awaiting fresh BEF reinforcements, as the reserves of conscripted men had to be dug ever deeper into. He had to conserve his infantry in the meantime, rely more on artillery bombardment, and concentrate on increasing tank support.

Ludendorff's Last Gamble, March to August 1918

At 4.40 am on 21 March, the Germans launched what was to be their last great offensive on the Western Front: Operation Kaiserschlacht.

General Erich Ludendorff
COS German Army,
circa 1917

It was divided into four sub-operations, Michael being the main assault, with the other three – Georgette, Gneisenau and Blucher-Yorck – designed as feints to draw Allied troops from the main attack.

The intention was to hit the Allied forces hard before the Americans tipped the balance with overwhelming numbers. Ludendorff had assessed that the quietest and therefore lightly-manned spot to commence was around the Somme. Opening with an artillery barrage lasting five hours, Ludendorff gambled that he could split the French and British forces by driving a wedge between them. He needed to subdue a weakened French force, riven with shortage-inspired mutinies, as well as a now weakened BEF, severely depleted due to unreplaced losses suffered in the failed Passchendaele offensive. This commanding position, although producing a more mobile warfare, was to peter out at the battle of Amiens in August. Ludendorff, in his war-diary, was to describe this turning-point as 'the blackest day in the German army's history'. It led ultimately to his resignation and dismissal in October. The end of the war was in sight.

Local servicemen's bravery awards

44648 Battery Sergeant Major Albert James Hill DCM, 25th Royal Field Artillery. Second son of the late Mr William Hill of Ironbridge. Killed in action in Flanders 22 May 1916. Had served twelve years in the army, five of which were in India. Before enlisting was in the employ of Mr. A. Corfield, late of Ironbridge and now of Shrewsbury, as a butcher. Age 32. The citation for his Distinguished Conduct Medal award reads, 'For consistent good work, notably when the battery and billets were heavily shelled, displayed great coolness and courage when removing the wounded at great personal risk.'

46631 Lance Sergeant William E. Owen MM. 15th Battalion, Durham Light Infantry. Son of Mr T. Owen, 154 Crompton Road, Handsworth; lived with grandmother in Ironbridge. Killed in action aged 19 in France on 24 August 1918. Joined the Ironbridge Company, KSLI (TF), in March 1914 and went to France in May 1916 after transferring to the Machine Gun Corps. Won the Military Medal one day and was wounded the next in October 1916. After recovering in hospital in France was sent back to England as being under age. Transferred to the Durhams and went back to France in April 1918.

CHAPTER 6

1918/19: Aftermath and the Ironmasters' Toll

'War does not determine who is right - only who is left.'
(Bertrand Russell, Philosopher 1872 - 1970)

End Game

The first day of the Battle of Amiens (8 August 1918) marked the opening phase of the 100-days Allied offensive that would ultimately lead to the ending of the war. It also marked the end of

Battle of Amiens – men of the BEF 13th Battalion – 8 August 1918

static warfare and the beginning of the armoured phase, with the Allies making steady progress, driving the Germans back at a daily average distance of two kilometres. By 10 August there were signs that the Germans were pulling out of the salient after losing 50,000 troops captured by the Allies. The Fourth Army had taken 13,000 prisoners with a further 3,000 taken by the French. It was to be a turning point in the war. The battle for Amiens was marked by a definite change of pace. After the swiftness of the opening months and the heady success at driving the Allies back to the Marne, the Germans were affected by the stalemate position arrived at at the end of 1914. On 26 October Ludendorff resigned in protest at the lack of support from high command, thus pre-empting the intention to dismiss him anyway.

Germany's surrender, armistice declared

Thirteen days after Ludendorff's resignation, on 8 November, a delegation of German government officials led by Matthias Erzberger, MP for the Centre Catholic Party, drove across the line to discuss an armistice.

After three days of negotiations, the armistice document was signed by the Germans and the Allies on the fateful day, 11 November, in Marshal Foch's railway carriage in the forest of Compiègne. Not only American servicemen but also BEF and Allied soldiers were still dying in skirmishes up and down the western front after the official 11am deadline.

General John Pershing CIC, AEF believed that the war should not have ceased with an armistice. He fervently believed that the Germans should have

Marshal Foch's railway carriage, forest of Compiègne, 1918

been pursued to the gates of Berlin and forced to sign a surrender. In answer to his detractors among the Allied cause, who wanted to quickly sue for peace via an armistice, Pershing offered this simple rebuttal: 'If we do not pursue this strategy, then our fight against Germany will have been for nothing and we will have to do this all over again.'

This prophetic statement was proved to be accurate when Germany started another world war twenty years later.

News of the Armistice reaches Ironbridge

The national daily newspapers shouted out the Declaration of Peace on their front pages in banner headlines. For the *Wellington Journal* however, the subject didn't quite merit the front page. The news column on page three was the reader's first notification. The following report, written in somewhat quirky language, dated 16 November, reads:

END OF THE WAR
ARMISTICE WITH GERMANY
This week has witnessed the opening of the last scene in the great world war. Only a short while since Bulgaria threw up the sponge to be followed within a few days by Turkey. Last week Austro-Hungary capitulated and on Monday [the 11th] was signed the armistice between the Allied Powers and Germany. But what a different Germany from that which four and a half years ago set out to challenge the whole world. Broken, dispirited, almost bankrupt, she has had to bow to the inevitable and today the clash of arms is no more. The last dramatic scene at Marshal Foch's Headquarters was preceded by an incident in Germany, the most galling, it may be conceived, that the Kaiser has ever experienced. No longer the despot of 1914, he has had perforce to yield up his crown; and his crafty son the Crown Prince, followed suit by renouncing all claim to the imperial dignity... The Kaiser and the Crown Prince have bolted to Holland and other crowned heads (ruling the confederation of states comprising the

crumbling German Empire) have also found safety in flight...
Prussia, the head of the empire, is in a state of revolution and
time will decide whether the monarchy will reside in another
family other than the Hohenzollerns.

The *Journal* also carried pictures of an impromptu gesture by
the Wellington Market Committee to clear the floor of the indoor
market so as to hold an Armistice tea party for the local children.

Similar parties were held across the nation as the period of
euphoria continued for quite a number of days. The factories in the
Ironbridge gorge proclaimed a half-day holiday at the announcement
but, with that over, it was back to business as usual.

Victory had been secured with Britain's empire intact. The
general feeling was one of relief. The war was over and those

Wellington Market Hall celebration, children's Armistice party

that had survived were now safe. Everyone rejoiced, but joy was tempered as the human cost was remembered. One in eight families had been affected by war fatalities, and the casualty list was to keep growing as the effects of the various weapons of war took their toll on servicemen.

Deaths caused by 'war effects'

This umbrella term covered many war-related ailments. For some Ironbridge-area casualties the war was destined never to be over. They had been maimed by ammunition or artillery fire, or new weapons such as poison gas, or they suffered the psychological scars of war. And there was not the range of remedial treatments or even antibiotics such as there are today.

The Wrekin Honour Roll records Ironbridge-area servicemen affected:

267822 Private George B. Davies, *6th Battalion Cheshire Regiment. Only son of Mrs & the late Mr. W.H. Davies, 12 Dale Road, Coalbrookdale. Died of wounds at the Royal Salop Infirmary, Shrewsbury, 4 October 1918. Enlisted in 1914 and had served one year in France when he was wounded on 30 July 1917, brought back to Northampton Hospital and then to the RSI. Dies age 24.*

136712 Private Harry Davis, *The Labour Corps. Husband of Mrs E.M. Davis, 54 Plane Street, Oldham. Son of Mrs Davis, Ironbridge. Died of wounds, Worcester Hospital, 6 March 1919. Buried in St Michael's, Madeley Churchyard, age 39. Formerly 53519 Devonshire Regiment.*

11593 Private Harry Hanley, *5th Battalion KSLI. Lived at Ironbridge. Died at the home of his brother-in-law Mr H. Dodd, Hodge Bower, Ironbridge, 1 December 1921 from effects of war. Wounded at the Battle of Loos 1915 and was brought back to England and spent 12 months in Brighton Hospital before being discharged from the army*

*in 1916 and had been in poor health since. Full military
funeral, buried in St. Michael's Church, Madeley. Died
age 34.*

Prisoners of war

From early on in the war thoughts turned to the plight of the
many servicemen who had been captured by the enemy during
the various battles. They were termed prisoners of war – PoWs –
and usually interned by the Germans for the duration. There were
limited means of repatriation, or willingness on the part of the
Germans to do so, as these men were deemed captured pawns
removed from the fighting deliberately to reduce the enemy's
fighting capability.

Out of a total of approximately seven million men held as
PoWs by all combatant forces over the period of the Great War,
Germany held two-and-a-half million. At the time, Germany
was divided into twenty-five Army Corps districts which each
controlled PoW camps either dotted across the battle fronts or on
home territory.

KSLI prisoners of war fund: The *Journal*'s campaign

From 1916 onwards in the UK there was a concerted effort to help
the nation's PoWs and various funds were set up under the provisions
of the War Charities Act 1916. In Shropshire the KSLI fund was
instituted to raise funds at home for the welfare of the men. The
KSLI, being the biggest local recruiter of men, the *Journal* got
behind its efforts and printed a series of releases reporting the known
list of captives and the KSLI fund's efforts to provide support for
them. The *Journal* of 22 June 1918 printed a half-page listing the
KSLI PoWs and appealing to readers to subscribe under the special
'Journal Subscriptions' option:

The King's Shropshire L.I. Prisoners of War Fund
Patrons: The Earl of Powis (Lord Lieutenant of Shropshire),
Sir John Cottrell, Bart. (Lord Lieutenant of Hereford)
President: Mrs Reade; Vice President: Sir Beville Stanier MP

Subscriptions List
Subscriptions for the above fund will be gladly received by the Editor of the Wellington Journal and Shrewsbury News *who will hand over the subscriptions each week to Mrs. Luard, Hon. Sec. and Treasurer of the County Fund. We decided to offer to run this subscription list, as we thought we might be able to appeal to Shropshire people in remote districts and all over the county who would otherwise not be reached in the ordinary way.*

Will you Help our Prisoners to Bear their Burden?
In accordance with the War Office Scheme started in December 1916, all Food Parcels for Prisoners of War have to be packed in authorised premises by certified packers. Mr. T.B. Butcher of 7, Castle Street, Shrewsbury has consented to act as packer for the KSLI. His work is entirely voluntary, as is that of the certified packers who assist him.

The *Journal* dated 20 July 1918 features another half-page detailing the progress of the KSLI PoW fund in banner headlines, sternly directing the reader to the article which opens with a letter to the editor:

READ THIS LETTER
Dear Sir – I should be glad to express to you and to those who have contributed to the fund through your columns, the thanks of the committee. If the need for help is realised I feel sure the £20,000 which will be required to provide our Prisoners from the KSLI Regiment with the bare necessities of life will be raised... £8,137 6s. 4d. was collected in Shropshire & Herefordshire from January 1st to June 30th 1918... This will supply 435 prisoners with food, books and clothes parcels... Louie Louard, Hon Sec & Treasurer

Ironbridge-area servicemen's PoW experiences

*12077 **Private James Edward Farlow**, 1st Battalion KSLI. Son of Mr & Mrs J. Farlow, 3 Waterloo Street, Ironbridge.*

Casselle (Cassel) PoW camp, circa 1915

Died of wounds as a prisoner-of-war in Casselle Camp, Germany, 19th July 1918.

This bare entry in the Wrekin Roll of Honour for the Ironbridge area belies the varying treatment received by James Farlow and other captured men in the war. Although not all PoW camps were located on German soil, it would appear James Farlow was held at a camp in Germany at or near Cassel (the spellings vary as the town changed its name to Kassel in 1928).

The German army's usual practice in the First World War was for the capturing unit to take them back up the line under armed escort to their base camp for onward shipment to their home base in Germany for incarceration in the nearest established PoW camp to their individual headquarters. The capturing unit would appear to have been from the XI Army Corps as their HQ was at Kassel/Cassel in the south-western province of Thuringia (east central Germany). German PoW camps were divided into officers' camps (*Offizierlager*) and servicemen's camps (*Mannschaftslager*). In the case of Farlow, as his rank was private he would have been detained in a camp located a few miles outside Cassel, possibly at Langensalza camp (previously a training facility established in 1914 and built to accommodate up to 10,000 men). The official website of the International Committee of the Red Cross (ICRC) lists no historical record for James Farlow as a PoW. This suggests that he had spent a short time at the camp as he was very recently captured and died from his wounds or complications arising, possibly made worse by the arduous trip from the frontline to Germany. Despite the Germans' notorious zeal for meticulous record-keeping, this may explain why a proper record card was not raised to detail Farlow's tenure at the camp and filed with the Red Cross which was standard procedure. His name would have been listed as a fatality and despatched with other similar records to the BEF in France within months of his demise in July 1918. He is listed on the Ironbridge memorial (with initial E shown instead of J – suggesting a preferred forename). His brother William, killed at Passchendaele, is also recorded on the monument, marking two of the fifty-three sons of Ironbridge town lost to the Great War.

A Madeley man's story: Major Charles Allix Lavington Yate VC

As we read in Chapter One, although an early VC winner, Major C.A.L. Yate reveals another courageous twist to his Great War story, concerning his PoW experiences. He was captured after defeat at Le Cateau on 26 August and imprisoned at Torgau camp in Germany where they tended his wounds.

After repeated attempts to escape, he was apprehended a few weeks later on 19 September by German factory workers who were suspicious of his civilian apparel. Fearing capture and the possibility of summary execution as a spy, he decided to commit suicide.

He died on 20 September and was buried at CWGC Berlin South-Western cemetery at Stahnsdorf, near Potsdam, Germany.

PoW casualties from the Ironbridge area

Against Geneva convention rules, some PoWs were put to work near battlefronts, as this evidence from the Wrekin Honour Roll testifies:

201178 Private Harold Douglas Jones, *1/4 Battalion KSLI. Son of Mr J.A. Jones, 16, Wesley Road, Ironbridge. Died in France while a prisoner-of-war in German hands, 6th July*

*Cenotaph, Whitehall, London –
opening ceremony, 1920*

*1918. Subsequently it was learned that he was killed while
being put to work in the front lines.*

The Cenotaph: A memorial of temporary permanence (1920)

Sir Edwin Lutyens was specially commissioned to construct a
temporary war memorial to the fallen in Whitehall, London, as a
focus for the 1919 National Peace Day commemoration ceremonies.
It was to be called the 'Cenotaph', meaning literally 'empty tomb',
decorated with wreaths and flags, fashioned in wood and plaster
made to resemble a solid block of stone. This temporary structure
was replaced by the permanent stone marker we see today, which
was formally unveiled upon completion by King George V in 1920.

The Ironmasters' toll: Ironbridge-area war casualties are determined

The official figures show that one in eight families across Britain had
lost a relative to the Great War. Every person in the UK had either
suffered personally or knew others who had. This sad fact prompted
a nationwide fever of commemorative monument building,
decorating public places such as town halls, market squares, village
greens and of course churches across the UK. Most were funded by

public subscription. The number and diversity of tributes erected locally and around the Ironbridge area is testament to just how heavy a price this small industrial town and its surrounding villages paid. These precious memorials recorded these 107 young men to be remembered always.

Great War memorials erected in the Ironbridge Area

The haste to build memorials across Britain after the war meant that some monuments erected were of varying quality, neither appropriate nor well-constructed. Fortunately this was not the case in the Ironbridge area where the observer is struck by the meticulous care and dignity of each. A measured pace seemed to have been applied, as in some cases, Ironbridge area in particular, they were still being built into the middle to late 1920s. Local memorials were erected by each village, with the larger commercial enterprises contributing.

Coalbrookdale
The Holy Trinity Church: Great War Plaque

This magnificently decorated Anglican church displays a wall plaque at the north end of the nave which lists all the dead of the

Holy Trinity Church: Great War plaque

Holy Trinity Church, Coalbrookdale

parish. Maurice Darby's name is on this plaque as well as on the main Coalbrookdale memorial. The church is the centre and managing church for the Coalbrookdale memorial as its original instigator.

Great War Memorial, 1921

Associated with Holy Trinity church, this memorial is located outside the gates of the former School of Science and Arts Institute (now a private house) at the junction of Wellington Road and the road fittingly called Paradise. This stone plinth, adorned with a cross, lists all the dead from the local area.

Maurice Darby is on this memorial. His father Alfred attended the ceremony as head of the Coalbrookdale company.

Great War memorial – Paradise, Coalbrookdale

Dedication ceremony, 1921

The *Journal* of 28 May 1921 printed a report of the inauguration ceremony. Here is an extract:

Coalbrookdale War Memorial

The unveiling and dedication of the handsome war memorial attracted a large crowd on Sunday afternoon... The memorial was made and erected by the Coalbrookdale Company, to a design by Mr. H. Fowler of Coalbrookdale... The inscriptions were:

'Their name liveth evermore'

below,

'Erected by public subscription in grateful memory of those named below who gave their lives in the Great War – 1914 - 1919'...

The proceedings commenced with a brief memorial service conducted by the Rev. C.B. Crowe, Vicar... The lesson was read by Colonel Woodland... The service over, a procession was formed, marshalled by Col. Woodland and proceeded as follows to the memorial: Rev C.B. Crowe and E. Roberts (Ironbridge), Major General Sir Charles Townshend MP,[7] Mr. Alfred Darby, Mr. W.S. Malcolm, Mrs. Darby, Col. & Mrs Whitmore[8] (Dudmaston), Miss Hunt, Miss Malcolm, members of the War Memorial Committee, Coalbrookdale Band, Ironbridge Comrades, Alderman Dyas, Corporation and mourners and friends... Mr W.S. Malcolm (Chairman) asked General Townshend to unveil the memorial... Rev Crowe dedicated it as F. Lloyd (Bandmaster) played the Last Post... Gen Townsend thought there was nothing so glorious for a man as to give his life for his country... Alfred Darby as Chairman of the Coalbrookdale Company here handed the deed of the site as a gift to the Borough Council... was accepted on behalf of the Madeley District Council by Alderman Dyas AB (Chairman).

---

7   Readers of our *Wellington in the Great War* in the same series will recall General Townshend's dubious wartime exploits and his fervour for unveiling post-war memorials.

8   Descendants of the famous Whitmore family, associated with the founding of the KSLI regiment at Bridgnorth – again, see *Wellington In the Great War.*

Maw & Co commemoration plaque, Pals company

Coalport & Jackfield
Maw & Co – Pals company, Great War plaques, c.1920

Inside the works site, housed in what was once the company offices, now private flats, is a hallway decorated with three panels made up of Maws tiles and detailing the list of employees who served in the Great War. Instigated by the company board it was erected in the 1920s by the workforce from specially designed tile product and meant to serve as a permanent reminder to successive employees of their comrades' sacrifice for the sake of their company, the king and the empire.

St Mary the Virgin Church: Great War memorial wall plaque

Coming under the Broseley parish, this Gothic-style brick and slate rendered C of E church complete with mini-steeple was erected in 1863 and designed by Sir Arthur Blomfield (maternal uncle and mentor of Sir Reginald who later designed the Menin Gate memorial). It is constructed of varied local brick and bears a passing resemblance to Keble College Chapel. The floors contain excellent examples of local tiles, and the sanctuary windows are claimed to be of the school of the Pre-Raphaelites. Some of the woodwork dates to the mid-1700s and was removed from an older chapel of ease. There are some exceptional examples of furniture from the 1600s.

St Mary the Virgin Church, Jackfield, Ironbridge

A commemorative decorated wooden plaque is placed on the western end wall about ten feet up listing the servicemen from the area who died in the Great War.

St Mary the Virgin Church, Great War memorial plaque

Coalport & Jackfield memorial footbridge, September 1922
Although a unique form of memorial, its practical purpose
of uniting two communities across a mighty river serves as a
permanent reminder to the user not only of its function but the
spirit of common loss shared by both. Its construction was paid for
by public subscription. The opening of the official war memorial
footbridge took place on 22 September 1922. A plaque was bolted
to the bridge which lists the twenty-six servicemen from the area
who died (including Privates W. Stephan and E. Colley of The
Lloyds, Jackfield). Commemoration ceremonies are held annually
at the bridge site on Remembrance Sunday.

Remembrance Sunday 2016, the Coalport and Jackfield bridge

Coalport and Jackfield memorial footbridge, opened 1922

Ironbridge – the war memorial in the square, March 1924

The Ironbridge memorial comprises three stone steps which lead up to a square base surmounted by a life-size figure of a soldier in full marching order. Three bronze plaques on the base bear the dedications and names of those who died in both wars. The memorial was not erected in its current position next to the bridge in its own paved area facing towards the town; it was originally sited across the road in the square directly across the Wharfage (being the main through road) facing towards the river. Colonel Sir Arthur Garrett (Shropshire Yeomanry), who was rumoured to have 'gone over the top' to face the enemy with just a walking stick and revolver – was invited to the town to unveil the official Ironbridge war memorial on 8 March 1924.

It was thought the city fathers originally wanted the memorial placed facing riverwards as a respectful reminder to all of the origins of the town and the significant part the river played in its development and prosperity.

Original Ironbridge memorial statue circa 1925. (Note position of figure – facing outwards)

Present site and position of memorial statue, Ironbridge

Madeley War Memorial, 1922

In 1922 the new Madeley memorial, a stone needle plinth, was unveiled by Lord Forrester and dedicated by local clergy. It was paid for by public subscription and originally located at the junction of Church Street and Park Street outside the Congregation Chapel (now the Maddox Physiotherapy Clinic). In September 1970 it was moved to its present position on Russell Green, being rededicated by the Reverend Jelbart.

Madeley Memorial, Russell Green

Rededication ceremony, Lavington Yate VC, August 2016

On 26 August 2016 a ceremony was held in Madeley at the official war memorial as part of the regional response to the official ongoing national First World War centenary commemorations. Representing Telford & Wrekin authority, Councillor Rae Evans was invited to attend the rededication ceremony where she laid a wreath on the newly laid stone recently added to the site. This stone is carved with the details of the VC winner Major Lavington Yate in celebration of this momentous event in Madeley's history. The stone was blessed and prayers said by Reverend Alan Walden.

The occasion was also attended by members of the local branch of the Royal British Legion who acted as a standard-bearing guard of honour. A bugler from Major Yate's regiment also attended and played the *Last Post* followed by the *Reveille* in tribute. This was a part of the programme of nationwide commemoration of the Great War's centenary and paid for out of Telford & Wrekin's Community fund.

Madeley rededication ceremony for Lavington Yate VC, 26 August 2016

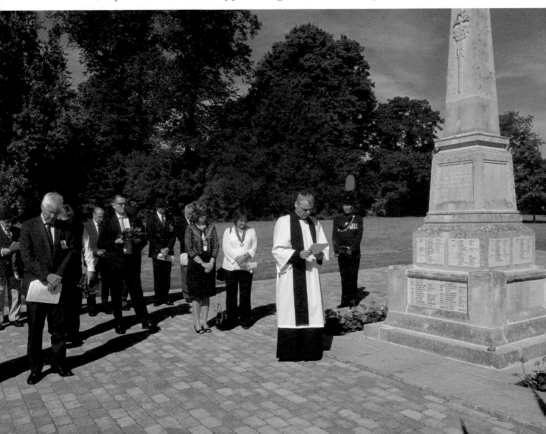

Madeley rededication ceremony 2016 – commemorative stone for Major Charles Allix Lavington Yate VC

Ironbridge Remembrance Sunday commemorations, November 2016

The author attended this commemoration ceremony which is marked annually with a ceremonial wreath-laying by the local branch of the British Legion. As is customary, a lone trumpeter

Above: *Ironbridge War Memorial, Remembrance Sunday, 2016*

Below: *Ironbridge commemorations: Remembrance Sunday, 2016*

played the *Last Post*. This was a fitting tribute to the fallen, made annually in this town now reduced to a mere hamlet of the city of Telford.

Although this once great hive of industry is now silenced, and the great Ironmasters' days are long gone, Ironbridge's place on the world stage remains secure. Over half a million visitors a year from all over the globe flock to this little town to view its metal bridge. They come to pay homage to a surviving monument of a once glorious past. This symphony in cast iron is a proud symbol marking the birthplace of the world's first industrial revolution in the UK.

The Ironbridge war memorial stands reverently in the shadow of its industrial history and is a fitting homage to all of the 107 sons of Ironbridge sacrificed to the Great War.

Above the Lych Gate memorial in Wellington is inscribed in gold lettering, 'Greater love hath no man than that he lay down his life for another.' This sentiment never more aptly applied to the men of Ironbridge and the surrounding Shropshire communities who answered their country's call in time of greatest need and paid the ultimate price.

They must never be forgotten.

Appendix

Comprehensive A-Z list of Ironbridge-area Great War casualties

66269 Private John William Adams
2nd Battalion, The West Yorkshire Regiment. Only son of Mr and Mrs Adam Adams of Ironbridge. Died of wounds France 25 April 1918, age 18. He had only been in the army for a few months and was mortally wounded after going overseas. Formerly worked for CWS (retail) and was a teacher at Madeley Wood Wesleyan Sunday school.

L/N 19725 Lieutenant John Spencer Ruscombe Anstice
Royal Fusiliers (City of London Regiment). Only son of Colonel Sir Arthur Anstice, formerly of Marnwood, Ironbridge. Died in the Dardanelles 2 May 1915, age 21. Educated at Eton and Sandhurst and was commissioned and gazetted into his regiment in September 1913 and on the outbreak of war was with his regiment in India. Went with the BEF to the Dardanelles and was killed in action.

S/11748 Private John Armstrong
5th Battalion, The Cameron Highlanders. Son of Mr Armstrong of 32, Wesley Road, Ironbridge. Killed in action at Loos, 25 September 1915. A member of Ironbridge church choir, he went to live with his sister at Hawick where he was an apprentice in the hosiery mills, but joined Camerons on the outbreak of war. Died age 21.

53534 Private Ernest Edward Aston
21st Battalion, West Yorkshire Regiment. Formerly 48333 Lancashire Fusiliers.

Born at Broseley, lived at Ironbridge, killed in Flanders 24 August 1918.

97752 Gunner Francis Arthur Aston
Royal Garrison Artillery. Husband of Mrs M. Aston, 41 High Street, Broseley. Son of Mr and Mrs Aston, 61 Wesley Road, Ironbridge. Killed in action in France 15 July 1917. Before joining the army was in employ of Messrs Smith & Son, grocers, of Ironbridge

26094 Private William Baugh
6th Battalion KSLI. Son of Mr and Mrs W. Baugh, The Lodge, Ironbridge. Died on 18 August 1917 from wounds received at Ypres (Passchendaele). Shot by sniper as member of Lewis Gun team. Age 19, worked at the Severn Foundry, Coalbrookdale. Buried at Dozinghem Military Cemetery, Westvleteren, Belgium.

41920 Private George Beddoes
2nd Battalion, The Worcestershire Regiment. Born and lived at Ironbridge, killed in action in France 17 April 1918. Enlisted in the Royal Warwicks and later transferred to the Worcesters.

763146 Private John Henry Benbow
28th Battalion, County of London Artists Rifles. Born and lived at Coalport. Killed in action in Flanders, 30 October 1917.

5468 CSM William E. Bennett
7th Battalion, KSLI. Husband of Mrs B.M. Bennett of 33, Hills Lane, Shrewsbury. Eldest son of the late Mr and Mrs Walter Bennett of Ironbridge. Died of wounds received at Ypres 3 April 1916. A regular soldier having served in the KSLI for nineteen years, spending most of his time in India until the end of 1914. Buried in a military cemetery in Poperinge.

16753 Private Alfred Bowen
3rd Battalion, Scots Guards. Son of Mr Edward Bowen of Coalbrookdale. Died of fever in Military Hospital, London, 18 September 1917. Belonged to Ironbridge Volunteers but was

in Buenos Aires when war broke out, returned and joined Scots Guards. Buried at Brompton Cemetery, Kensington.

43044 Driver Arthur Bowen
Royal Field Artillery. Son of Mrs A. Bowen, 21, Coalport Bridge, Coalport. Died of heatstroke at Baghdad, Mesopotamia, 23 July 1917.

WR/207074 Sapper John Bowen
Royal Engineers, Born at Jackfield. Died at Salonika, 6 September 1918.

12449 Private Francis Joseph Bowers
1st Battalion, KSLI. Only son of Mr and Mrs Bowers. Born at Sutton Wood, lived at Ironbridge. Killed in action at the Battle of the Hindenburg Line, 24 September 1918.

200321 Private George Bradley
1/4th Battalion, KSLI. Born and lived at Jackfield. Killed in action at Cambrai, 19 April 1918

21324 Private Frederick Branford
1st Battalion Royal Warwickshire Regiment. Husband of Mrs N. Branford of Aston, Birmingham, but formerly of 23, Madeley Road, Ironbridge. Killed in action in Flanders, 18 April 1917. Was a regular soldier and was a despatch rider during the war.

203588 Private William Edward Brazier
4th Battalion, King's Shropshire Light Infantry. Lived at Ironbridge. Previously reported wounded and missing but later confirmed died of wounds received on the Aisne, 31 May 1918. A cross in his memory was presented to St Luke's Church Ironbridge on 29 October 1922 by Mr and Mrs W. Cooper.

327085 Private George Brickley
The Labour Corps. Husband of Mrs. E. Brickley, 80 Wesley Road, Ironbridge. Died in Royal Herbert Hospital, Woolwich,

17 November 1918. First man from Madeley to volunteer for the forces. Enlisted in the Royal Field Artillery. Had seen much action in the Dardanelles and in the Serbian retreat. Escaping wounds, he was attacked by influenza, followed by pneumonia, from which he died. Military funeral at home and buried in St. Michael's churchyard Madeley. Age 25, was formerly a baker employed by a Mr Woodhouse.

G. Broadhurst
Commemorated on Ironbridge memorial, but unable to find out any more information about him.

45259 Private Harry Burton
Royal Defence Corps. Son of Mrs E. Burton, Station Hotel, Ironbridge. Died at Military Hospital Oswestry, 4 July 1917. Buried at Broseley Cemetery.

30399 Private Reginald Burton
1st Battalion, King's Own Royal Lancaster Regiment. Son of Mr E. Burton, Station Hotel, Ironbridge. Brother to Harry. Killed in action in Flanders, 12 October 1917. Commemorated on Tyne Cot Memorial, Passchendaele. Died age 35.

16642 Private Edward Colley
8th Battalion, KSLI. Son of Walter Colley, 48, Coalford, Jackfield. Killed in action Salonika 18 September 1918.

130308 Pioneer William Henry Coombes
1st Battalion, Special Brigade, Royal Engineers. Husband of Mrs M.E. Coombes of Coalbrookdale. Killed in action in France, 25 June 1916.

14785 Lance Corporal William George Colin Cooper
1st Battalion Bedfordshire Regiment. Son of Mr C.W. and Mrs M.A. Cooper, 17 Dale Road, Coalbrookdale. Killed in action at Hill 60 Flanders, 5 May 1915. Severely wounded by a grenade and had to be left in the trench owing to gas. Age 23, member of

Coalbrookdale brass band and was formerly employed at the Saville Club, Piccadilly, London.

25510 Private William Edward Cornes
5th Battalion. KSLI. Son of Mr W.E. Cornes, The Lloyds, Ironbridge. Died of wounds in France, 11 September 1917, age 19. Was formerly employed at the Coalbrookdale works and joined KSLI in November 1916.

200185 Private Arthur Cullis
1/4th Battalion, KSLI, of Madeley Road, Ironbridge. Born and raised in Ironbridge. Killed in action at Cambrai, 30 December 1917.

8996 Private Cecil Davies
2nd Battalion, KSLI. Eldest son of Mr E. Davies, 26, The Wharfage, Ironbridge. Killed in action at Hill 60 Ypres, 25 April 1915. Enlisted in 1908, served for four years in India and had seen action in all the engagements in which his battalion had been involved.

267822 Private George B. Davies
6th Battalion Cheshire Regiment. Only son of Mrs and the late Mr W.H. Davies, 12 Dale Road, Coalbrookdale. Died of wounds at the Royal Salop Infirmary, Shrewsbury, 4 October 1918. Enlisted in 1914 and had served one year in France when he was wounded on 30 July 1917. Brought back to Northampton Hospital and then to the RSI. Age 24.

136712 Private Harry Davis
The Labour Corps. Husband of Mrs E.M. Davis, 54 Plane Street, Oldham, and later of Ironbridge. Died of wounds at Worcester Hospital 6 March 1919. Buried in St Michael's Madeley churchyard, age 39. Formerly 53519 Devonshire Regiment.

52042 Private Charles Dorricott
4th Battalion, North Staffordshire Regiment. Born and lived at Ironbridge. Killed in action in France 14 October 1918.

3548 Private Frank Sorton Downing
2/6th Battalion, Royal Warwickshire Regiment. Husband of Mrs. A. Downing, Wellington Road, Coalbrookdale. Eldest son of John Downing, 23, Dale End, Coalbrookdale. Died of wounds in France (the Somme) 1 July 1916. Age 26, he enlisted in November 1914, prior to which he was a cabinetmaker employed at Birmingham. Former bellringer at Coalbrookdale Parish Church.

31983 Private Frederick Drewball
7th Battalion, KSLI. Husband of Mrs Lucy Drewball, 36, Newbridge Road, Ironbridge.
   Died in France 14 November 1918. Buried Plot 5, Row C, Grave 27, Abbeville Communal Cemetery Extension, France.

204800 Private Bertie Edwards
1/5th Battalion, Yorks & Lancs Regiment. Born and lived at Jackfield. Killed in action in Flanders, 22 October 1917.

37156 Lance Corporal Thomas Edwards
2nd Battalion, The King's Own Yorkshire Light Infantry. Son of Mr and Mrs Edwards, 31, Walker Street, Hoylake, Cheshire, formerly of 'Woodlands', Ironbridge. Killed in action in France 30 September 1918. Had been employed as a porter at Madeley Station.

23735 Private William Henry Edwards
7th Battalion, KSLI. Born at Madeley, lived at Ironbridge, killed in action at the Battle of Ancre, Somme, 13 November 1916.

21069 Private Horatio Ellis Evans
7th Battalion, South Wales Borderers. Eldest son of Horatio William Evans, The Lloyds, Ironbridge. Killed in action in Salonika, 17 September 1918, age 32.

12077 Private James Edward Farlow
1st Battalion KSLI. Son of Mr and Mrs J. Farlow, 3 Waterloo Street, Ironbridge. Died of wounds as a prisoner of war in Casselle Camp, Germany, 19 July 1918.

8995 Private William Farlow

5th Battalion, KSLI. Husband of Mrs Lily Farlow, Eriviat Lodge, Denbigh. Eldest son of Mr and Mrs J. Farlow, 3 Waterloo Street, Ironbridge. Killed in action at Ypres 21 October 1917. He had served seven years in India and three in France. Brother to James Edward.

5556 Private George Goodall

2nd Battalion, The Prince of Wales's Leinster Regiment (Royal Canadians). Son of Mr and Mrs Goodall, 200, Wergs, Jackfield. Killed in action in Flanders, 19 October 1918.

200993 Sergeant Jack Goodwin

5th Battalion Tank Corps. Lived at Coalbrookdale. Killed in action at Flanders 16 April 1918. Formerly 15580 in the KSLI and in the Machine Gun Corps. No known grave, commemorated on Ploegsteert Memorial, Belgium.

27760 Private William Edward Hall

Border Regiment. Son of George Hall, Sycamore House, Ironbridge, later of 15, Church Hill, Ironbridge. Killed in action on the Somme, 18 November 1916. Formerly a moulder at Coalbrookdale Works. He joined the colours on 8 March 1915 and had only been in France for six weeks. Considered one of the best bowlers in the Ironbridge District League. Age 26. Formerly 4996 Herefordshire Regiment.

11593 Private Harry Hanley

5th Battalion KSLI. Lived at Ironbridge. Died at the home of his brother-in-law Mr H. Dodd, Hodge Bower, Ironbridge, 1 December 1921, from effects of war. Wounded at the Battle of Loos 1915, brought back to England, spent twelve months in Brighton Hospital, discharged from the army in 1916, and remained in poor health thereafter. Full military funeral, buried in St. Michael's Church, Madeley. Age 34.

32793 Private William Hanley
6th Battalion, KSLI. Born and lived at Ironbridge. Killed in Action at the Battle of Menin Road, 20 September 1917.

19266 Private Edwin Harris
1st Battalion, KSLI. Only son of Mr and Mrs Harris, Church Hill, Ironbridge. Killed in action at Hill 70, Cambrai, 12 October 1917. Formerly employed by Mr W. Bishop of Posenhall.

15332 Private Archibald Heighway
2nd Battalion, KSLI. Son of S. and E. Heighway, 9 The Lloyds, Ironbridge. Died in UK, 30 October 1918. Had served four years in the KSLI. Age 24. Buried at Madeley Churchyard.

44648 Battery Sergeant Major Albert James Hill DCM
25th Royal Field Artillery. Second son of the late Mr William Hill of Ironbridge. Killed in action in Flanders 22 May 1916. Had served 12 years in the army, 5 years of which were in India. Previous to enlisting was in the employ of Mr A. Corfield, late of Ironbridge and now of Shrewsbury, as a butcher. Age 32.

54928 William Edward Howells
10th Battalion, Royal Welsh Fusiliers. Lived at Ironbridge. Killed in action in Flanders, 26 September 1917.

10036 Lance Corporal George Hurdley
1st Battalion, KSLI. Lived at 3, Chapel Road, Ironbridge. Killed in action at Ypres Salient, 31 January 1915. Had been in the regiment for two years prior to the war and at the outbreak was serving in Tipperary, but was soon in action at the front. Shot in the arm and stomach. Age 21.

222440 Private John Hurdley
The Labour Corps. Third son of Mr and Mrs T. Hurdley of 3 Chapel Road, Ironbridge. Died of wounds in France, 24 August 1918.

Enlisted in 1915 and had taken part in the Dardanelles operation. Returned and went to France where he died from wounds received from a bomb blast. Prior to enlistment was employed as a barman in Bilston, West Midlands. Brother to George.

70289 Private Albert Joseph Jones
Royal Welsh Fusiliers. Lived at Ironbridge. Died of wounds received in Flanders, 5 November 1917.

201178 Private Harold Douglas Jones
1/4 Battalion, KSLI. Son of Mr J. A. Jones of 16, Wesley Road, Ironbridge. Died in France while a prisoner-of-war in German hands, 6 July 1918. Subsequently it was learned that he was killed having been put to work in the front lines.

53133 Private John Jones
19th Battalion, King's Liverpool Regiment. Born and lived at Jackfield. Killed in action in Flanders, 12 October 1916.

F/ 13493 Air Mechanic, 2nd Class, Joseph Jones
Royal Naval Air Service. Son of Mr Joseph Jones, The Lloyds, Ironbridge. Missing presumed dead, 9 August 1917. Had passed examinations for Clerk to Surveyor of Taxes but volunteered for the RNAS instead.

3021 Private Wilfred Ray Jones
1/6th Battalion, South Staffordshire Regiment. Born at Coalbrookdale. Killed in action in France, 9 April 1915.

8011 Private Ralph Thomas Kendall
Royal Scots Fusiliers. Husband of Katherine Kendall of 9, Woodside, Coalbrookdale. Died of wounds at Rawalpindi Hospital, Boulogne, France, 1 July 1915, age 33.

19837 Private Cecil Lucas
10th Battalion, KSLI. Born in Ironbridge, lived in Wellington, killed in action at the Battle of Épehy, 18 September 1918.

Corporal Herbert J. Marshall
New Zealand Expeditionary Force. Son of Mr Marshall, stationmaster at Coalbrookdale. Killed in action before 28 August 1915 at the Dardanelles. Came over with the NZ contingent, but some years previously was a pattern-maker at Coalbrookdale Works. He was a member of the Ironbridge Rowing Club having won the Kynnersley Cup for sculling. Unable to trace final details. Age 33.

73816 Bombardier Harry Millward
B Battery, 235th Brigade, Royal Field Artillery. Third son of James Edwin and Eliza Millward, 49, Wellington Road, Coalbrookdale. Killed in action in France, 29 March 1918. Had been wounded three times and had suffered from enteric fever. Was in the retreat from Mons. Before enlisting had been a member of the Ironbridge Territorials. Age 23. Buried at Foncquevillers Military Cemetery. Brother to James.

201247 Private James Millward
1/4th Battalion, KSLI. Husband of Mrs Millward of Coalbrookdale, son of James Edwin and Eliza Millward, 49, Wellington Road, Coalbrookdale. Died of wounds in France, 7 January 1918, age 26. Buried at Rocquigny-Equancourt Road, Military Cemetery. Brother to Harry.

244683 Guardsman Frank Morgan
4th Battalion Grenadier Guards. Second son of Mr Thomas Morgan, 22 Woodside, Coalbrookdale. Died in hospital in UK, 23 March 1918, age 27. Buried at Coalbrookdale Church Cemetery.

31758 Private Benjamin Morris
The Prince of Wales's Volunteers (South Lancashire Regiment). Lived at Coalport. Killed in action near Armentières, 25 December 1916.

50416 Private Cecil Morris
2nd Battalion, The Prince of Wales's Volunteers (South Lancashire Regiment). Lived at Jackfield. Died of wounds in Flanders, 27 April 1918.

200200 Private William Joseph Mullard
1/4 Battalion, KSLI. Eldest son of the late Mr Charles Mullard of Coalport, brother of Mrs Owen, Park Lane, Madeley. Died from pneumonia in hospital in France, 23 June 1918. Joined the army in 1912 and at the outbreak of war was drafted to India and China and later to France. Died age 24. Formerly worked at the Coalport China Company.

7284 Private George Nicholas
1st Battalion, KSLI. Son of Mr Joseph Nicholas, St Luke's Road, Ironbridge. Died of wounds in France, 25 August 1915. An army reservist and had been in the fighting area ever since war began. Lived with his brother and worked as a dyer at the Hope Works, Ramsbottom, Lancashire, prior to his enlistment. Died age 31.

94630 Private Samuel Nickless
1st Battalion, The King's (Liverpool Regiment). Brother of Mr Harry Nickless of Lincoln Hill, Ironbridge. Killed in action in Flanders, 27 September 1918. Formerly 44217 The Prince of Wales's Volunteers (South Lancashire Regiment).

K/14764 Stoker First Class Thomas W. Nickless
Royal Navy. Son of Mr Samuel Nickless, 30, Lincoln Hill, Ironbridge. Killed in action on board HMS *Acasta* at the Battle of Jutland, 31 May 1916. Had served four years in the Navy and although his ship was not sunk, he was one of six killed on board. Previously worked for the Coalbrookdale Company.

21289 Private William John Norry
1st Battalion, KSLI. Son of Mr W. Norry, 2 Wellington Road, Coalbrookdale. Killed in action on the Somme, 22 March 1918. Was wounded at Hooge in October
1915 but recovered and returned to the front. Before joining the army was employed at the Severn Foundry, Coalbrookdale.

11452 Private George Oakes
6th Battalion, KSLI. Son of Mr George Oakes of Coalbrookdale.
Killed in action at Ypres, 13 September 1917. Killed by shell while
asleep. Age 42, was employed as a moulder by the Coalbrookdale
Works before enlisting.

7791 Private Albert Oakley
1st Battalion, KSLI. Born in Broseley, lived at Jackfield. Killed in
action at Ypres, 4 November 1914.

11602 Corporal William Onions
5th Battalion, KSLI. Son of Mr I. Onions of Coalbrookdale. Killed
in action at Arras 8 April 1917. Enlisted in the first month of the
war, was sent to France May 1915 and was wounded in August
1915. After five weeks in hospital at Yarmouth had five days leave
and in October returned to France. Before enlisting was employed
at the Coalbrookdale Works and was a member of the Hodge Bower
Bowling Club. Died age 29.

6969 Private Benjamin Owen
11th Battalion, The Sherwood Foresters (Notts & Derbys Regiment).
Born at Dawley, lived at Ironbridge, killed in action in Flanders,
30 July 1916.

200324 Private Robert Owen
7th Battalion, KSLI. Son of Mr W. Owen, 18, New Bridge Road,
Ironbridge. Died of wounds in France, 24 October 1918.

46631 Lance Sergeant William E. Owen MM
15th Battalion, The Durham Light Infantry. Son of Mr T. Owen,
154 Crompton Road, Handsworth; lived with grandmother in
Ironbridge. Killed in action in France, 24 August 1918. Joined
the Ironbridge Company KSLI (TF) in March 1914 and went to
France in May 1916 after transferring to the Machine Gun Corps.
Won the Military Medal one day and was wounded the next in

October 1916. After recovering in hospital in France he was sent back to England as being underage. Transferred to the Durhams and went back to France in April 1918. Was a scholar at the Bluecoat School and before enlistment was employed at the Severn Foundry, Coalbrookdale. Was a member of Ironbridge Choir for six years. Died age 19.

2600 Gunner William Henry Pace
Royal Field Artillery. Eldest son of Mr and Mrs H. Pace of Strethill Lodge, Coalbrookdale. Died of dysentery in Mesopotamia. Volunteered in March 1915, went to India and then Mesopotamia in 1916 where he came through some of the severest fighting in the retaking of Kut and several other engagements. He was then sent to Palestine in 1918 and was in the big offensive in September. Died in hospital in Alexandria age 28. Buried at Damascus. Brother of Mrs D.G. Colley, Parville House, Crescent Road, Wellington.

135624 Private Bertie Reginald Perry
1st Battalion, Canadian Mounted Rifles. Elder son of Mr Samuel Perry, Woodside, Coalbrookdale. Killed in action in France, 15 September 1916.

Z/ 3806 Signaller Cyril William Phillips
Royal Navy Volunteer Reserve. Son of Mr and Mrs J. Phillips, Heathcote, Madeley Road, Ironbridge. Killed in action in HMS *Gurkha*, 8 February 1917. Formerly in the office of the borough surveyor and up to the time of joining the Navy was an articled pupil to Mr George Riley, engineer and surveyor to Wellington Urban Council. Memorial service held at St Michael's, Madeley, on 19 February 1917. Died age 20.

200253 Sergeant George Plant
1/4 Battalion, KSLI. Born at Ironbridge, lived at Madeley, killed in action at the Battle of the Welch Ridge, Cambrai, 30 December 1917.

4/8381 Private Edwin Pugh
2nd Battalion, The Prince of Wales's Own (West Yorks Regiment). Lived at Ironbridge. Died of wounds in Flanders, 4 December 1916.

200932 Private George Henry Pugh
1/4th Battalion, KSLI. Son of Mr T. Pugh, 36, Westley Road, Ironbridge. Killed in action at the Battle of Bapaume, 25 March 1918. Joined the army in 1914 and after service in China returned with the Territorials to France.

09566 Second Lieutenant Herbert Ernest Randall
7th Battalion, KSLI. Eldest son of Mr and Mrs John Randall, 15, Wellington Road, Coalbrookdale. Died of wounds at Locon, Béthune, 29 May 1918. Joined the army in 1915 and had been in France since December 1917. Educated at Coalbrookdale Secondary School and for many years played the organ at the Wesleyan Chapel. Died age 23.

28458 Sergeant Arthur Reynolds
The Depot, The King's (Liverpool Regiment). Husband of Mrs Nellie Reynolds, 252 Werps Road, Jackfield. Died at home from war effects, 3 November 1920. Buried in Broseley Churchyard.

31122 Lance Corporal George Reynolds
6th Battalion, South Staffordshire Regiment. Son of Sergeant Arthur Reynolds. Husband of Mrs A. Reynolds, 252 Werps Road, Jackfield. Killed in action at Regina Trench, Thiepval, France, 21 October 1916.

12685 Sergeant Samuel Rich
6th Battalion, KSLI. Born and lived at Woodside House, Coalbrookdale. Killed in action at Ypres, 23 September 1917. Uncle to Mrs G. Hanley, 4 Stretton Close, Sutton Farm Estate, Shrewsbury.

42927 Private Harry Rickers
The Queen's (Royal West Surrey Regiment). Lived at 7, The Woodlands, Ironbridge. Died at home from the effects of gas, 17 August 1921. Worked as a baker for Mr Bagnall, Beaumont Road, Ironbridge, before enlisting. After a military funeral was buried at St. Michael's Church, Madeley. Age 33.

34189 Private William Roberts
10th Battalion, KSLI. Born and lived at Jackfield. Died of wounds in France, 23 August 1918.

12207 Private Thomas Rogers
6th Battalion, KSLI. Son of Mrs Rogers, Ironbridge. Killed in action at the Somme, 30 June 1916.

349508 Gunner Allen Sands, Canadian Royal Artillery. Youngest son of Mrs Sands, 55 Church Hill, Ironbridge. Killed in action in Flanders 29 October 1917. Had served three years six months in the Royal Navy and fought in the Battle of the Falkland Islands in 1914. Later joined the Canadian Royal Artillery. Before enlisting was a member of St Luke's church choir. Age 19.

115256 Private Henry Smallman
35th Battalion, Machine Gun Corps (Infantry). Son of John and Elizabeth Smallman, 25, Belmont Road, Ironbridge. Killed in action in France, 26 March 1918, age 21. Buried at Pozières (Somme) British Cemetery. Brother to John Charles.

16756 – Private John Charles Smallman
18th Battalion, The Lancashire Fusiliers. Husband of Mrs Sarah Ann Brierley (formerly Smallman) of 12 Hey Top, Greenfield, Oldham. Son of John and Elizabeth Smallman, 25 Belmont Road, Ironbridge. Died at Brighton Hospital of wounds received in France, 21 November 1918, age 28. Buried in St. Michael's, Madeley. Brother to Henry.

14394 Sergeant Richard Everard Buckworth-Herne-Soame
The Depot, KSLI. Elder son of Sir Charles Buckworth-Herne-Soame, 5 Cherry Tree Hill, Coalbrookdale. Died of wounds at Kempston Hospital, Eastbourne, 30 July 1916. Seriously wounded in action he was brought back to hospital at Eastbourne but succumbed to his wounds. After a military funeral was interred at Ocklynge cemetery. Age 24.

9226 Private Alfred Speake
2nd Battalion, KSLI. Second son of Mr T. Speake, 15, Lincoln Hill, Ironbridge. Died of wounds received at Ypres, 2 March 1915. Had served four years in India and was then drafted with his regiment to France. While fighting in the trenches he was shot and died a few hours later. His brothers Percy and Harry who were in action nearby assisted in his burial.

Harry Speake
Commemorated on Ironbridge War Memorial and brother to Harry and Percy – unable to trace further information.

4036 – Private Percy Speake
9th Battalion, The Royal Warwickshire Regiment. Son Mr T. Speake, 15, Lincoln Hill, Ironbridge. Killed in action in Mesopotamia, 19 April 1916. Joined the Royal Warwicks soon after the outbreak of war. Died age 23. Brother to Harry and Percy.

24064 Private Frederick Stephan
2nd Battalion, KSLI. Youngest son of Mr E. Stephan, The Post Office, Coalbrookdale. Brother of Mrs Boland, Postmistress, Coalport. Killed in action in Salonika, 31 October 1916. Killed instantly with a bullet through the heart. Was a painter before joining the army and worked for Mr Blocksidge of Madeley and Mr E.J. Wilcox of Ironbridge.

36893 Private William Harry Stephan
1/4th Battalion, The Loyal North Lancashire Regiment. Born and lived at Jackfield. Killed in action in Flanders, 18 July 1917.

200640 Lance Sergeant John Steventon

1/4th Battalion, KSLI. Son of Mrs Steventon, Bath Tavern, Ironbridge. Killed in action at the Battle of Bligny, 7 June 1918. Joined the Ironbridge Territorials, went out to India with them and was later drafted to France. Had been in the army 3 years 9 months when he met his death. Before joining up he played centre-forward for Ironbridge Football Club.

33296 Private Harry Swinton

3rd (Garrison) Battalion, The King's (Liverpool Regiment). Born and lived at Ironbridge. Died at home from war effects, 4 March 1917. Formerly 18502 KSLI.

7227 Private Edward Thomas

1st Battalion, KSLI. Born and lived at Ironbridge. Killed at the Battle of Hooge, Ypres, 9 August 1915.

9652 Guardsman Robert Watson

King's Company, 1st Battalion, Grenadier Guards. Husband of Mrs Watson, St Luke's Road, Ironbridge. Died of wounds in France, 12 October 1915. Before rejoining his regiment, worked as a moulder at the Severn Yard, Coalbrookdale. Died age 34.

9938 Private Henry Welch

1st Battalion, KSLI. Son of Mr T. Welch, Wesley Road, Ironbridge. Husband of Mrs H. Welch, 15 Church Hill, Ironbridge. Died in the UK from pulmonary tuberculosis due to gas poisoning, 16 September 1920. A regular soldier he joined B Company of the KSLI in 1911 and later transferred to Kitchener's Army. Father to Mr H.T. Welch who lived at 1, New Road, Ironbridge.

Alfred Whitehead

Royal Navy. Son of Joseph Whitehead, head baker at Iron Co-op Wholesale Society. Lost at sea on HMS *Queen Mary* at the Battle of Jutland 31 May 1916. Joined the Navy before the war and after leaving the training ship HMS *Impregnable* was transferred to the *Queen Mary*. Died age 17.

90956 Private Arthur W.J. Wilde

4th Battalion, The King's (Liverpool Regiment). Commemorated at Coalbrookdale War Memorial. Son of Mrs A. Wilde, Benthall Villa, Broseley. Killed in action in France 16 April 1918.

15753 Private Joseph Wilde

7th Battalion, KSLI. Born and lived at Ironbridge. Killed in action near Arras 13 May 1917. Age 38.

205477 Private Arthur Ferriday Wilkes

15th Battalion, The Sherwood Foresters (Notts and Derbys Regiment). Son of Mrs Wilkes, 57, Madeley Road, Ironbridge. Died from wounds in Hospital at Étaples in the presence of his mother, 23 May 1918. Formerly 200629 of the KSLI. Brother to Mrs Keay, The Shrubbery, Madeley Road, Ironbridge.

44519 Private Thomas Williams

1st Battalion, Prince Albert's (Somerset Light Infantry). Lived at Jackfield. Died of wounds in Flanders 30 August 1918. Formerly 13315 of the KSLI.

39958 Private Richard Frederick Cyril Wood

12th Battalion, The South Wales Borderers. Born at Albrighton, lived at Ironbridge, killed in action in Flanders on 22 November 1917.

17950 Private William Ambrose Wright

5th Battalion, KSLI. Husband of Mrs Margaret Wright, 6 Ladywood, Ironbridge, formerly of Madeley. Killed in action at the battle of Delville Wood on the Somme, 23 August 1916. Before enlisting worked as a tile-presser at Messrs Prestage's Works, Jackfield. Died age 42. Left a widow and seven children.

41565 Private John Wyld

18th (4th Glasgow) Battalion, Highland Light Infantry. Born at Jackfield, lived at Ironbridge, killed in action in Flanders, 19 August 1917. Formerly G/23700 South Staffordshire Regiment.

Second Lieutenant Frederick Charles Youden

15th Battalion, Australian Imperial Forces. Formerly a captain in the 4th Battalion, King's Shropshire Light Infantry. Third son of Mr and Mrs John Youden, 3, Beechwood Drive, Jordanhill, Glasgow, formerly of Madeley. Killed in action at Gallipoli, 8 August 1915, age 33. Commemorated at the Lone Pine Memorial.

Index